To: Dr Karen Ke...

May this
Heal broken Hearts,
Mend Relationships
And Restore Hope
to All that Study this Book.

Rev. *[signature]*, Ph.D. AMS

WHO? ME! ANGRY?

WHO? ME! ANGRY?

Rev. Dr. Jerry Campbell

Copyright 2011 Rev. Dr. Jerry Campbell
ISBN 978-1-257-77590-3

PREFACE

It is a joy to share my research, education, and knowledge in the field of anger and its management, as well as, the emotional feelings of one of the seven deadly sins. It is my desire for the reader to get to know their own emotions and to be able to learn to manage the emotions of anger. This book is written as a workbook and is designed for the reader to mark and underline important ideas and to answer self revealing questions.

Over the years, my staff and I have taught anger management skills to over 3,000 adults in the state of Georgia. In 1995, the state of Georgia's Department of Human Services approved a manuscript that I worte for the teaching of anger management to parents that were suffering with domestic violence.

Like all books, to read a book from cover to cover is like walking down a street and kicking a used tin can. While chasing the can and kicking it once in awhile you may find a gold ring. That gold ring keeps us kicking the can. So while you read this book you may find something of worth.

Some of what I share you may think is not relevant. In time, the golden ring will jump off the page. You then have something of value that maybe used in anger management. It is my wish for you to use these golden rings found to make a difference and will give tools to manage anger.

FOREWORD

The essential material for this book has grown out of studying many courses and of personal experiences. There have been many counseling sessions, numerous seminars and years of personal research and study on the subject matter. At all levels of professional training there have been essays written, debates on this universal emotion, and at times very deadly behavior.

What is anger? I have found that each person have their own definition for anger. Yet there are some words that appear to cling to the term "anger." Some of these words I have used to demonstrate the different levels of anger. From simply being upset to being completely out of control, anger is a problem for us all.

While anger is listed as one of the seven deadly sins, our world does not consider anger as just one subject manner for theology. I have found that there are studies of anger in most every profession and field of study known.

My study of anger began in theology. The Bible tells us to "be angry and sin not." The world tells us to refrain from domestic violence. Some have learned the police will arrest you for being angry. The world warns us about what is called "deadly passion behavior."

This book is a "self-help" style book. I encourage you to incorporate the knowledge you learn in this workbook into your daily life and thus, overcoming any negative anger behavior.

I am most grateful to everyone who has given many valuable suggestions. There have been many individuals that have given the encouragement to write this book. I say "Thank you," to all.

SPECIAL THANKS TO:

Margaret Brock – Rossville, GA

Kevin Campbell – Ringgold, GA

Kelli Campbell – Rossville, GA

Kraig Campbell – Rossville, GA

Nancy Campbell – Rossville, GA

Eugene Coleman – Ft. Oglethorpe, GA

Billie McGraw Crosby – Lompoc, CA

Brenda Elder – Lookout Mtn, GA

Mark Elder - Lookout Mtn, GA

Jennifer Keith – Ft. Oglethorpe, GA

Mark Neal – Chattanooga, TN

James Neal – Chattanooga, TN

Gene Pole – Chattanooga, TN

Denny Whitesel – Ft. Oglethorpe GA

DEDICATION

I dedicate this book to the memory of my parents: Sam and Marguerite Campbell who were married from June 1933 until the death of my father some 54 years later.

My father, Sam Campbell (02/14/1907 to 07/29/1987) lived to be 80 years old. For his use of logic, common sense, and outstanding provisions for my daily needs and care I can never repay. And for his wisdom that he shared with me as a child and as a young man. His honesty and truthfulness in conducting his business and life as a man's man was heroic. I was truly blessed with a special person as my father. His knowledge of "no" was at times unspeakable as I could see it in his eyes. I know there could not have been a better person! My father came out of an Eastern Kentucky Coal Mine accident as a man that was disabled. With limited benefits, he worked long hard hours in order to give me a wonderful life-style. This man I called, "Dad."

My mother, Marguerite E. (Beatty) Campbell (11/17/1911 to 05/19/2004) lived to be 93 years old. For her kindness, dependability, skills in teaching by both words, and deeds. For having the ability of knowing exactly what I needed at the right time. In our home it was necessary for her to work full time. Therefore, she worked long hours to provide for my needs as her third and last child. This lady I called "Mom."

Mom was a shy lady who enjoyed teaching a lady's Sunday School Class every Sunday morning. Publically, she did not like to draw attention to herself. But, her thoughts were not only from the mind, but from her heart. After her death I found the following poem written in her own handwriting. The poem did not have a name as she never planned for it to be published. So I named it "Instead." In the words of my mom that she wrote on May 25, 2000:

"INSTEAD"

"Now instead of fear, there is calm
Instead of defeat, there is victory

> Instead of doubt, there is assurance
> Instead of being hid in a place
> I am hidden in Christ"

    I never heard my parents argue, call each other names, hit each other or do anything that to cause each other problems. As they both worked together to make life enjoyable for each other and my brother, sister and myself. Both my parents were people of faith. I can say it was a joy to be reared in my household.

TABLE OF CONTENTS

Introduction		xv
Chapter One:	Upset!	1
Chapter Two:	Miffed!	9
Chapter Three:	Frustrated!	15
Chapter Four:	Afraid!	23
Chapter Five:	Mad!	29
Chapter Six:	Angry!	39
Chapter Seven:	Fight!	49
Chapter Eight:	Rage!	61
Chapter Nine:	Irrational!	71
Chapter Ten:	Out of Control!	79
Chapter Eleven:	Hot Buttons!	89
Chapter Twelve:	Whatever! – So What?	109
Chapter Thirteen:	The Secret!	129
Campbell's Anger Flow Chart:		145

INTRODUCTION

Originally, I wrote materials for anger management seminar and training for the Department of Family and Children Service of the State of Georgia. The manuscript was taught to their clients over a period of six years.

After writing this manuscript I thought that I had an average understanding of being angry. While studying Clinical Pastoral Education (CPE) at Erlanger Regional Hospital in Chattanooga, Tennessee it was pointed out that I might have an anger problem too. May response was: "Who? Me!"

CPE is an in-depth study of for individuals studying for the ministry. Therefore, it was then that I began my personal and professional study on anger and how to management it. I never considered myself to have anger issues. After all, anger was an issue that everyone else had but not me! Therefore, I had a good degree of anger and was in the state of denial.

It was in 1996 that the manuscript was written. At that time I had an undergrad B. A. degree in Behavioral Science and Psychology from Tennessee Wesleyan College and a Master's Degree in Pastoral Care and Counseling from Clark-Atlanta University. While enrolled in a Doctoral Degree program at Erskine University in Due West, South Carolinian I believe I had a good understanding of anger and its management. To be honest, I now know that I was so wrong for I had so much more to learn. During my Ph. D. studies at The American International University I became to know that I knew very little about anger and its influence.

I knew that there were some words that appeared to be "hot buttons" and statements that would cause anger issues to explode. I continued to live my life with its joys and disappointments. This of course brought both happiness and anger issues.

After an auto accident in 2005 and a long medical recovery process, I and my family suffered from Post-Tarmac Stress Disorder. I knew that (PTSD) and negative medical conditions will bring anger issues. I also knew that a person maybe angry and not know why. Not feeling worthy may cause a person to be angry. There are so many areas of unresolved issues that might lead a person to feel angry that I do not have room here to list them all.

I have learned to find the cause of your anger and you are on your way to solving your personal anger issues. Once you have an understanding as to why you are angry, then you can start to find ways to be in control of your life. However, I do not believe that we are able to bring our anger to a complete stop.

While anger like happiness is a gift, it is one that must be better understood and used for the betterment of our life and others.

I have attempted to use "reason" in writing this book. In the Torah or Old Testament from Isaiah 1:18 we may read and learn the following lesson: "Come now. And let us reason together, said the Lord." My father was what I would call a "simple man." He had a third grade education and would be considered "under-educated" today. But in his simple life-style, he would ask: "Does it make sense son?" Or if he was a little upset, I could hear him forcefully ask: "Don't it make horse sense?"

To make "common sense" out of anger is what I believe is in order while studying our anger issues. Let us come and reason together about the changes in our life, society and relationships. So, it is from this perspective that I approach the subject of anger.

CHARTER ONE

UPSET!

I was told when I was a small and very young little boy that "sticks and stones may break my bones but words will never hurt me." This is a lie. It is wrong, wrong, wrong! Words do hurt! They hurt for a life time! Bones for the most part will heal in a short period of time. With broken bones we move on and often forget most of the details about the event. But hurtful words linger in our memory for a lifetime.

Words have a habit of staying with us. In the back of our mind the words stay. And those words keep on repeating over and over. The pain continues to hurt as we are able to visualize these events. So what do we do? How do we protect ourselves from the pain of words?

The pain of words may cause emotional damage that if not dealt with may stay and influence everything we think and do for the rest of our life. It is simply called baggage. Being upset is the first step in developing baggage from the hurt of words.

The word "upset" has many definitions. One is that of being emotionally agitated or disturbed. Another definition is that of being overturned and being in disorder. When referring to being upset as you become angry you are suffering from being distressed and having other emotional feelings. In this chapter we look at being upset.

We all have experienced it. We all have caused it. When will we ever learn to stop it? When will we ever learn to handle it? These are all great questions that I hope we will be able to discuss.

Also, we have been taught to turn the other cheek when someone offends us. I have just recently heard that when one turns the other cheek after being offended be prepared to be hit with their other fist. Is that the real world that we now find ourselves living in? I believe you can relate to these experiences.

According to Plato there are two things a person should never become upset at, "what they can help, and what they cannot." While in any relationship, we will develop stored up emotional energy that maybe both positive or negative. This emotional energy comes in many and varied actions and reactions that at times will be demonstrated by physical action.

There is always a relationship between who we are and what we believe we are. Being "upset" is one of those emotions that we have a habit of storing up, covering up and holding on to until we may justify releasing the energy. One of the most upsetting emotions that we handle is "lying." When someone lies to you it triggers a negative emotion that you may be able to control and store. Or you might not and we will release this energy as we feel is necessary.

No one wants to be lied too. I have never found anyone that has told me that they enjoy having anyone lie to them. It is just not an enjoyable experience. So I often wonder why someone ever lies. They may "win" at the moment but in time it will be exposed. To lie is to be untruthful, to bear a false statement or witness. Lying is very upsetting to anyone. This brings unhappiness, disappointment or distress because the one person that we have some level of trust in has told us an untruth.

Our anger spews out when anyone lies to us. We cannot stand to be lied too! However, we first lie to ourselves. And for some reason we are able to handle it when we lie to ourselves. Any story you tell yourself about as to who you are any belief you have and any feeling you are aware of is an object of your consciousness. You, in your essence, are always something that experiences all these and remains more complete than any of them. When you realize that you are inherently larger than any feeling that enters your consciousness you develop this very awareness. This awareness will change the feeling, and it will release its grip on you.

Likewise, any ideas that you have about yourself are all relative and who we feel ourselves to be and who we really are. This is in ourselves an awareness that is necessary for us to correctly evaluate who we are and what makes us tick.

In each individual I find there are three elements. I would like to call them persons but that might not be correct. What I am talking about is the "me" person, the "I" person and the "myself" person. Now you know what I mean. Me, myself, and I are those three elements or essences that live within our mind, body, soul or spirit.

I compare these three in one as to the Trinity of God. The Trinity as it is a part of the belief of the Christian faith; God the Father, God the Son, and God the Holy Spirit.

As we become more aware of ourselves we will learn how to gain control of our feelings. Our feelings are important to us. Our emotions and feelings as to who we are and what we are affect our daily living and life-style. We will learn that being out of control from being happy to being out of control from being upset drives us down life roads on our journey.

In awakening to this self-me relationship, we begin to be present with our experience in a new way. We learn to consciously hold our thoughts and feelings in our own larger fields of awareness. Then, even if we are troubled and confused, this nonreactive quality of presence to ourselves allows us to restore ourselves to a sense of wholeness. This is the power of awareness.

What makes a person upset? That is a great question to ask. And it is a great area of our life to take a good look at. Have you ever wonder why we get angry over the smallest things and blow up and why we blow it totally out of proportion?

Why do we get angry at the people we love and care about? Anger can appear to be irrational but if you learn to look below the surface you will find the real causes of anger. When we find the real causes we then can successfully overcome our anger.

So we must develop some awareness that may allow us to see what causes our anger. When we start taking charge of our emotions we may be able to stop getting upset and being angry.

For instance we find that our day is not going as well because we are thinking about something that has been upsetting. Let's say your boss/spouse/parent yelled at you this morning in front of everyone. That was a blow to your ego! But do you need to let it upset you any further?

Always feel the love in your heart when you make your decision to make sure that when you decide what is going to upset you and what isn't, then you've taken control.

What is upsetting to you?

1. _____
   _____

2. _____
   _____

3. _____
   _____

What isn't upsetting to you?

1. _____
2. _____
3. _____

There is a Chinese Proverb that reads: "If you are patient in one moment of anger, you will escape a hundred days of sorrow."

Have you ever had those hundred days of sorrow? If so, list them.

1. _____
2. _____
3. _____

Dr. Joyce Brother stated that "anger" repressed can poison a relationship as surely as the cruelest words."

Can you list just a few poison relationships?

1. _____
2. _____
3. _____

Who do you think needs to control your feelings when someone or something is upsetting you?

1. _____
2. _____

3. _____
   _____

To come to the emotional level of being upset is the first step toward becoming angry. Often we are able to skip a whole series of steps and go on to being mad, angry or completely out of control. In other words going from zero to sixty in a split second when we become upset.

Can you list a few times that you have become upset?

1. _____
   _____
2. _____
   _____
3. _____
   _____

From the words of Aristotle, "Anyone can become angry. That is easy. But to be angry with the right person, to the right degree, at the right time, for the right purpose and in the right way…that is not easy."

Being upset and angry is not all bad. It is how we react to these upsetting issues or persons. The Bible tells us to "Be angry and sin not." I have always thought that we should teach our children never to be angry, but teach them how to be angry. An unknown author wrote: "The best answer to anger is silence." That is hard to do.

Can you list some other way of teaching?

1. _____
   _____
2. _____
   _____
3. _____
   _____

It was Will Rodger that once said, "People who fly into a rage always make a bad landing." So it is easy to see that most of us have a difficult time when it comes to being angry. To continue to be upset and to feed our anger is what makes our clear mind seem clouded. How many hard landings have you had?

Can you list some?

1. _____
   _____
2. _____
   _____
3. _____
   _____

Ambrose Bierce said it may be best for us to "speak when you are angry and you will make the best speech you will ever regret. How often have you spoken by simply being upset at the moment and forever have regrets?

Hopefully, after reading this book you will learn a few ways of reminding yourself of your place on the emotional flow chart, and be able to stop, look and listen to your emotions and make the necessary changes before you move on to the danger zone.

How much more do you suffer from being upset and grieved, than from those very things for which you are upset and grieved?

In other words, according to Marcus Aurelius, "How much more grievous are the consequences of anger than the causes of it?"

It is not hard to get upset at anytime for anything. We most often get upset with ourselves more than with others. I have counseled so many times with individuals that are beating up on themselves. So if we are not upset at others we might just get mad and angry at ourselves

Have you ever gotten mad at yourself and if so, list why?

1. _____
   _____
2. _____
   _____
3. _____
   _____

What are the things that you get upset and angry with yourself about?

1. _____
   _____
2. _____
   _____

3. _____
   _____

As we continue, let's be reminded of the words from St. Francis De Sales that reads; "There was never an angry man that thought his anger unjust." May I ask you, are you that person? Being upset is your first step that might lead to going deeper in the emotion of being angry.

As we become upset there is a physical reaction as our muscles begin to tighten up just a little. We also experience being a little depressed. We then become a little bit unhappy. We now will notice that our self-esteem is low and getting lower. We might even get a light headache.

Can you list some of the times that you have had these emotional and physical feelings?

1. _____
   _____
2. _____
   _____
3. _____
   _____

At this point, normally none of these events in our life are treated, repaired or fixed. So over time and even at early childhood these measures add up and are fed by more unresolved "stuff" and now our life is full of "stress." My heart doctor advised me that his patients do not die from strokes or heart attacks. They are killed by stress!

Can you list three of your most stressful issues?

1. _____
   _____
2. _____
   _____
3. _____
   _____

As a counselor I have been told that our services are too expensive. But the client never evaluates the funds they spend daily or weekly in the form of (drinks, drugs, entertainment, hobbies, etc.) in an effort to self medicate. Over a life time a person's "stuff" builds and builds. The building blocks form an "Ice Burg." The stuff becomes a life time of baggage. The baggage forms an "Iceberg." We become "cold." The tip of the personal "iceberg" is what most clients come into my office for "fixing." They are in complete denial of the real problems and when I attempt to go to that area of their life they conveniently stop the sessions.

Below the water level is where our clients need to focus. But these issues have been frozen so long and hard that chipping at it is all but impossible. Young children also have "icebergs" but are just smaller. We all have them. They never seem to go way and we struggle daily with dealing with our issues. There are two areas I would like for you to think about now.

Can you list the "tip of the iceberg?"

1. _____
   _____
2. _____
   _____
3. _____
   _____

Secondly, can you list some of you baggage that is below the frozen water line?

1. _____
   _____
2. _____
   _____
3. _____
   _____

It is no wonder as adults we become "cold" to things in our life and in our relationships. Have you ever thought or said, "That person is really upset?" only to realize that you know that person very well. Who? Me!

Being upset is a score of 10 according to Campbell's Anger Flow Chart. Others may name it something else. Whatever you may call it for me it is the first emotional step away from being happy and toward 60 the score of being angry.

CHAPTER TWO

MIFFED!

As we become "sulky" or "moody" and have been offended, a long walk maybe the remedy for our short temper. We easily become tiff over the smallest of petty and trivial quarrels. A tiff is a miffed. This is what I call the second step of emotional feelings that leads us to being frustrated, mad or angry and if miffed could result in us completely losing it all!

Can you list some times that you have experienced the emotions of being miffed. When was the last time you were sulky or moody?

1. _____
   _____
2. _____
   _____
3. _____
   _____

One of the thousands of reasons that may cause you to react by being upset and miffed is when someone lies to you. A lie is a lie! The trust factor has been broken. There remains a need to second guess and to doubt what is being told to you by that person. All my life, I have heard of someone telling "little white lies." There is no such thing as a "little white lie." Unless there is a little white person that cannot tell the truth!

Can you list some of the "little white lies" that someone has told you lately?

1. _____
   _____

2. _____
   _____

3. _____
   _____

We all know that mirrors don't lie. What you see is what you get. The only thing that is wrong is that the image is backwards. The right is on the left and the left is on the right. However, we adapt to this almost instantly. One of our most personal and important subjects that we become upset and miffed about is our physical appearance.

Can you list some of the things that you notice each morning as you look in your mirror?

1. _____
   _____

2. _____
   _____

3. _____
   _____

Your physical appearance is your outward sign. Your face is the focal point of that sign. The next detailed focal point is your eyes, **noise**, and ears. [*NOSE*] When going out to meet the public you wash your face and hands more than any other part of your body. It is so easy for you to get upset and miffed at your appearance. Most people for some unknown reason are not happy with their external appearance.

If you could make any changes in your appearances what would they be?

1. _____
   _____

2. _____
   _____

3. _____
   _____

I have seen a female family member that became so miffed at "doing her eye liner" that she threw the eye liner paint brush in the trash can in a split second. I think it is reasonable to state that our appearance is of upmost important to most of us. Giving attention to your personal appearance is one of the first activities of each day. Personal hygiene and your personal appearance both may drive you into a state of being angry. Therefore, you may become angry before you ever see another human being. It is real easy to have a "bad hair day!"

Anger issues may be more than the experiences that you have in your relations with others. Your family relations will suffer greatly if you wake up on "the wrong side of the bed!" We all know what that means. You may justify your anger by offering many excuses. Therefore, you never get to the cause and the root problems that cause you to be difficult to live with and angry most of the day.

Emotionally, being miffed may quickly allow you to move to the emotional level of frustration. Your emotional maturity might become tested. Part of the emotional growth patterns are dependent upon your experiences, knowledge, and the baggage you still lug around. You may have a need to be and to have others that are emotionally supportive during your life. This stability will help to have control over the issues that you face. You must come to know yourself and become accountable.

Can you list three things about you that is good or positive that no one else knows.

1. _____
   _____
2. _____
   _____
3. _____
   _____

To learn more about ourselves it is times like this where we need to identify what makes us act and react. Our emotions are one of the driving forces behind our energy that leads to anger. It might be of importance for you to get to know your emotions. Your emotions should develop in parallel with our age. In other words, when you become an adult we put away childish things. You are to act like an adult and not a small child or baby. Emotional maturity is necessary to being successful in relationships. Will you list the last few times you were a child in an adult body?

1. _____
   _____
2. _____
   _____
3. _____
   _____

Emotional immaturity is often seen as couples who have been physically attracted to each other come to the place in which the veil of romance has been lifted. The thrilling feel of chemistry has been removed. What is the relationship like once off the dance floor? What is the emotional status once the bills are due and there is not enough money honey? This quickly leads individuals to look at each other and wonder what happened. Because now, that sweet little lady or that handsome man is not only upset, miffed and frustrated but is getting mad and angry too! In another term, the dance is over!

Can you list any times in your life when you came to know that the dance was over?

1. _____
   _____
2. _____
   _____
3. _____
   _____

You may become miffed just by the decisions that another person makes that has an influence on your life. After the exciting whirlwind of parties and romantic dates that had swept each other off their feet and a decision to simply pay one bill over another one you may discover the anger level to increase. A person may become miffed when the other person makes a non-reversible decision without discussing it.

Has this ever happened to you? If so, please describe.

1. _____
   _____
2. _____
   _____

3. _____
   _____

Anger may make you feel that you are in a mismatched relationship. I have heard clients tell me that "she just doesn't understand me." Or "he makes all these decisions and then tells me about them afterwards and I can't stand it anymore!" The wedge begins to drive itself between the two and anger goes from zero to sixty in a split second.

What was the last wedge that was driven between you and your spouse, mate or friend?

1. _____
   _____
2. _____
   _____
3. _____
   _____

As a counselor we acknowledge this as the beginning of the breakdown of the relationship. You may claim that it is the result of poor communication. People grow apart from each other and wonder what happened?

What was the last "What happened" moment that you had?

1. _____
   _____
2. _____
   _____
3. _____
   _____

As you develop room in your emotional level for being upset and miffed, frustration comes forward easily in your emotional maturity. When you continue to feed these emotions and allow them to stew your anger level will rise quickly. However, if you will identify these different levels of emotions and claim them for your own, you might be able to stop your words and your physical actions before they go deeper into the level of rage.

Can you list a few ways in which you can come to a stop, check yourself, and not allow yourself to get out of control? It is called being in control of one's action. Or it may be just being mature.

1. _____
2. _____
3. _____

Are you emotionally mature or do you still have some truck size baggage? How do you relate to others? How do you relate when things don't go your way? How do you react when there is no money in the house? How do you act when you lose your job? It has been said that "when things get tough the tough get going." Are you a person with tough emotional traits?

Please list some of your personal tough traits.

1. _____
2. _____
3. _____

At this point in becoming angry you have moved a little far toward the emotional level of anger. Your problems seem to add up somewhat more. Your headache has now moved down our neck and into our shoulder or back. Your muscles ache and over the counter aspirin doesn't work anymore. Your relationships become more strained. Your "stuff" appears to become overwhelming. After all we are really miffed!

Have you ever thought or said, "That person is really miffed?" only to realize that you know that person very well. Who? Me!

Being miffed gives you the score of 20 according to Campbell's Anger Flow Chart. Others may call it something else. Whatever you may call it, it is the second emotional step away from being happy and you are on your way to being angry if you continue to feed your negative emotions.

CHAPTER THREE

FRUSTRATED!

Frustrated is an emotion that causes us to be discouraged and feeling exasperated. We feel completely unsatisfied. We become offended and annoyed often about nothing. The more we hurt others the more we become hurt ourselves. It becomes a" merry go round" type lifestyle. According to Albert Einstein, "anger dwells only in the bosom of fools." His statement is strong but it is not wrong?

We often are annoyed by those that love us the most over little things that "just drive us crazy." Often it is all about nothing. Or possibly over things that we do not understand completely and doesn't make sense. My medical doctor recently shared such an experience that he encountered.

I enjoy talking with my doctors. I attempt to get to know them as much as they will allow. I was sharing some of my thoughts about this book not knowing that he would give me "some food for thought." The "food" was not from him but from his grandmother who is still living back in his home country. This is what he said.

"I enjoy talking with my grandmother who still lives back in my home country. She insists on writing me. I tell her, "Mom you can call me anytime and we can talk all you want so why do you still write to me?" Her response was, ""Son, sometimes my fingers need to talk. You know they are attached to my heart and I need to write. So I write!" How great is that?

While he was having these emotional feelings of becoming frustrated with his loving grandmother because she would not simply call him. And when he questioned her, she lovingly defused his negative emotions of being frustrated. The wisdom that she taught him will remain with him for his entire life and no doubt he will past this family knowledge on to his children.

Can you list some of the ways that you think you could use in defusing frustration?

1. _____
   _____
2. _____
   _____
3. _____
   _____

Being frustrated or angry is like being under the influence of drugs or alcohol. It prevents us from rationalizing and thinking logically. Our anger maybe feed by a combination of an irrational perception of reality and having a low frustration point.

Frustration and anger both are a natural response. You have every right to be angry, but should learn to keep the anger in check. Being able to keep our emotions in check may be of greatest value in our life. Yes, greater than stocks, bonds, real estate, safety deposit boxes or any other items we might think has high value.

What are some of your frustrations that you know will cause you to become angry?

1. _____
   _____
2. _____
   _____
3. _____
   _____

None of us create frustration and anger in the same way. Each person has different beliefs and interpretations that produce emotions in our own individual way. We often have similar patterns. Only through awareness will you be able to see your own individual pattern. The question is, are we willing to change them?

When you gain the awareness of how the different elements operate and apply some effective tools and techniques for change, you can eliminate the cause of your frustrations and unhappiness that lead to anger. After all it was Marcus Aurelius that stated, "How much more grievous are the consequences of anger that causes of it?"

Are you able to list some of the consequences of your anger?

1. _____
_____
2. _____
_____
3. _____
_____

We need to become more aware of what makes us frustrated.

Can you list how you think you may become more aware of being frustrated and angry?

1. _____
_____
2. _____
_____
3. _____
_____

George Jean Nathan stated, "No man can think clearly when his fists are clenched." I have often wondered why we clench our fists as we become more frustrated and angry. It is part of our physical reaction to our emotional feelings. As a former pastor in the Christian community, I was once told by a lovely gray headed lady who had been in this church all of her life that "we are not an emotional church." I think I know what she was attempting to communicate to me. But that statement has been filed in the back of my mind and it comes out once in a while. Therefore, I look for the emotional level of a person, group, business, church or institution. For without emotions it or we are dead. We must have emotions or we become lifeless.

One of the many avenues in our life that contributes to our frustrations and anger could be our lifestyle. Most often, no one is really happy with their life or lifestyle. We are always attempting to change who we are, what we are and how we go about doing things. This within itself causes frustrations.

Can you name some of these proposed changes that give you frustration?

1. _____

2. _____

3. _____

Are you thinking about making changes in your personal life, relationships, work, or career?

If so, list some of the actions that you need to complete in order to make this change.

1. _____

2. _____

3. _____

Throughout this book keep in mind that it is your workbook. This is a book that requires individual response and hopefully causes you to take a look at yourself. This may require some action. As you work though this book it is my hope that you will actually make these changes. Keep in mind these are changes that you already want and believe you need.

What are some of your behaviors that you would like to make some changes?

1. _____

2. _____

3. _____

If we do not identify the areas of changes we will never move toward making them. These changes may be enough to make you frustrated. Therefore, we might become angry and not really know why. Nor will anyone else understand our anger issues. You see, the anger issues and frustrations remain hidden.

Are you willing to share some of your hidden areas of frustrations?

1. _____
2. _____
3. _____

Your leisure time and activities may cause you to feel different levels of frustration. Your energy level or lack thereof may also lead to depression. Once we become upset, miffed and frustrated our energy level begins to drop and here comes a small dose of depression. If depression is not identified and we fail to deal with it, we will swing into being stressed.

Now that was somewhat simple! Just being upset and miffed will bring on frustrations and then stress. It is real easy to simply allow our "stuff" to grow into major problems in our life. Without any other influence, we may jump from being miffed to being angry in a split second.

Have you ever done this? If so, make a list.

1. _____
2. _____
3. _____

An example of this is with finances. This is a hot bed for most couples. One person maybe a spender while the other saves or one is financially responsible while the other plays catch-up with all other bills. Who do we trust with our financial information? And above all, who do we trust with our plastic cards?

Who do you trust with your plastic cards?

1. _____
2. _____
3. _____

If you think that we may trust others with our wallet you may become very disappointed quickly. Often, we find that we cannot even trust the ones closet to us. Place your plastic in the hands of you darling child and see what happens. It would be wise for you to keep a closed eye on your monthly statements. When your little dear charges more than allowed and you are over the limit you can bet that your emotions will run wild. Don't be surprised if you find yourself frustrated or maybe really mad and angry.

Can you list some of the times that you have had this experience?

1. _____
2. _____
3. _____

There are so many ways a person may get to your wallet. Your wallet is not only your billfold but is the bank accounts, your retirement funds, your plastic cards and even your cash in your hand. When we fall for someone else needs and allow ourselves to be used, it is impossible to stop our emotional tsunami. Please, I hope you are not dirt dump! Being what I call dirt dump is to allow people like hired help, so called life-long friends or even the one you have just fallen in love with use your wallet!

List some of the tsunami in your life:

1. _____

Rev. Dr. Jerry Campbell 21

2. _____

3. _____

We might need to become aware that in reality we cannot trust ourselves. Many times I have felt like kicking myself. No wonder we walk around mad!

Can you list some of the times that you have wanted to kick yourself?

1. _____

2. _____

3. _____ *PETER*

We might take a lesson from the Apostle (Paul) [PETER] who said, "Silver and gold I have none, but that which I have I will give." He was talking about sharing the gospel with others. But if we take another look at what Paul is saying is that, "I am broke!" He was saying "I have no money." Or maybe he was saying: "Don't ask me to pay your bills."

How do you feel after being sucked into paying someone's bills or giving to others and leaving yourself short?

Can you list some of your emotions? Are you upset, miffed, frustrated, mad or angry?

1. _____

2. _____

3. _____ *Peter*

I know that theologically, Paul [Peter] is attempting to share the Gospel and to let others know that there is more to life than money. He is saying that to know the Gospel is far better than silver and gold. This is something that we have long ago forgotten. Do you agree or disagree with Paul's statement and why?

1. _____
_____
2. _____
_____
3. _____
_____

    I have at times believed it would have been better if I had told my others, "Silver and gold I have none, but that which I have I will give." They would have then known that I really didn't have any money.

Can you list away that you may be able to tell others that you are broke?

1. _____
_____
2. _____
_____
3. _____
_____

    Another emotion in our anger is the inward anger. Often we struggle within dealing with our frustrations. We beat ourselves up over and over again. In doing so our heart becomes colder and colder. A personal iceberg develops. This iceberg collects and gets bigger and bigger. The tip of the iceberg is an expression of being on edge. There appears to be a frown on our face and we lose our smile. We lose the happiness that is within. Depression really moves in quickly and our self-esteem drops to the floor. We become afraid to do anything for fear that we might become a failure in life.

    The pain of life sets within. When feed by depression and anger physical pain develops.

    Have you ever thought or said, "That person is really depressed and afraid?" Only to realize that you know that person very well, Who? Me!

    Being frustrated places you on the score of 30 according to Campbell's Anger Flow Chart. Others may name it something else but whatever you may call it, it is the third emotional step away from being happy.

CHAPTER FOUR

AFRAID!

After dealing with our emotions of being upset, miffed, and the frustration we often become afraid. The fear we experience is because of the unknowns. Unknowns result in worry. We worry and fail to trust ourselves and others. Not trusting ourselves and others is a self taught education. Being afraid of the things that we are worried about will often lead us into a state of madness.

I call this madness as Americans have been taught to be a believer. Now for the moment I'm not talking about a person's religion, but about the basic faith in our ability to deal with challenges. There is a trust in the basic faith in things as simple as believing that the sun will rise tomorrow. We know the sun has risen usually before 8 am each day whether or not we can see it.

For some reason when we become frustrated we "lose it." All abilities to reason leave. All common sense leaves the human being. All logical thinking that we have used all of our life is gone. As result insecurity sets in until we settle down.

Have you ever been told to settle down? If so, when was the last time and what was the reason?

1. _____
   _____
2. _____
   _____
3. _____
   _____

Have you stated that you're afraid of losing your job? Have you ever said, "I am afraid that I will fail?" Have you ever thought that you just could not do it? And after we were successful in not losing our job or falling apart, we got mad, at ourselves!

Being afraid is a distressing emotion aroused by impending danger, evil, pain, whether the threat is real or imagined; the feeling or condition of being afraid. Being afraid is a strong, unpleasant emotion and sometimes it is uncontrollable. Being afraid is our emotion of fear. Being afraid and the fear it brings is caused by actual or perceived danger or any threat that we think may happen.

Can you list any threats that you have felt?

1. _____
2. _____
3. _____

A very famous quotation concerning being afraid is "The only thing we have to fear is fear itself!"

Can you make a list of some of your fears that you know will cause you to be frustrated, mad or angry?

1. _____
2. _____
3. _____

How do you feel after experiencing strong fearful emotions? How did it leave you? Where you mad or in a rage?

Did it leave in feeling paralyzes?

1. _____
2. _____

3. _____
   _____

Being afraid is an emotional fear. Fear maybe a distressing emotion aroused by a perceived threat. Being afraid is a basic survival mechanism that we respond to as a stimulus such as pain or the threat of what we think is danger.

Can you list some of the times in the past that you have felt a threat that you would consider dangerous?

1. _____
   _____
2. _____
   _____
3. _____
   _____

Being afraid brings on other emotional feelings. Anxiety and agitation appear to live within the emotions of fear. The fear factor leads to being afraid. Some panic attacks are the results of the presence of fear and a feeling of imminent danger. We may succumb to this emotional condition and come to a state of not being able to function.

Can you list some of the times that you have experienced the state of not being able to function?

1. _____
   _____
2. _____
   _____
3. _____
   _____

However this emotional disorder is the doorway to most other emotional and mental diagnose Anxiety and agitation all begin with simply being upset and then feeding that level of anger.

Being afraid can also be an explosive emotion. Most animals when they feel forced into a corner will come out fighting and being aggressive. This behavior is the result of being afraid. We are no different! We too become agitated and will become both physical and verbally aggressive. Unfortunately, we are not able to experience being agitated and being aggressive over being hurt without being angry. The hurt is usually the result of being disappointed.

Can you list some of the things that make you feel disappointed?

1. _____
2. _____
3. _____

Being afraid, agitated, and aggressive brings an emotional feeling of anger. In the Bible we read: "Be not afraid for I am with you!" So is it a sin to allow ourselves to fall in the trap of being afraid, anxious and aggressive?

What do you think?

1. _____
2. _____
3. _____

Being afraid is an emotion that is again often overlooked within our emotional stability. One of our goals in life is to be emotionally stable. You are not able to get a gun if your background check shows signs of you being emotionally unstable. Society has a corporate fear of individuals that are not emotionally stable. Again it all comes down to the trust factor. Is this person emotionally stable and trust worthy?

Being afraid and fear swings open the door to most all other emotional and mental health issues. Happy and happiness are opposite of fear and being afraid. They both are parallel emotions headed in opposite emotional directions with opposite results.

How have both being happy and being afraid affected you?

1. _____
   _____

2. _____
   _____

3. _____
   _____

Usually the next emotional demise is what I call blooming depression! We cannot be depressed without fear and being afraid. An example babies maybe born sick and with birth defects but are not born with fear, being afraid, mad, angry or depressed. Babies are not born in a rage, out of control or irrational. So, how do we grow into this state of emotions?

It is just like math as it adds and multiplies. And we have learned to stuff it. For a short period of time it is the tip of the iceberg. As we continue to feed our negative emotional life it goes on beneath the water line..

Can you list what is at the tip of your iceberg at the present time?

1. _____
   _____

2. _____
   _____

3. _____
   _____

This area is often overlooked but has a tremendous impact on your life. One would not even begin to think that fear and being afraid is the root of our emotional instability. Yet fear and being afraid is based on one's values and faith system. This includes the big values such as honesty, integrity, loyalty, views on family, religion and our spirituality. Our life goals and the treatment and care of others are all a part of our emotional psyche.

Our mind is capable of altering the state of reality, consciousness or universal feeling and we can become afraid of everything or anything. We are able to bring ourselves to a state of depersonalization. We can best describe this during war time. We depersonalize the enemy. When we reach this state of mind and the fear that it brings we become desensitized and experience derealization. We call this being "shell shocked." We are able to bring ourselves to the point of being shell shocked and never have served in the military or in a war. Abuse and family violence is capable of people living in the state of being "shell shocked."

In an effort to build a support system it is important to have friends and family members that we can trust. Have you ever had someone that you consider a true friend? Would you say this person is trustworthy? Do you believe this person or people will always be there for you in a pinch?

Can you make a list of these people?

1. _____

2. _____

3. _____

Have you ever thought or said, "That person is really afraid?" only to realize that you know that person very well. Who? Me!

Being afraid places a person on the score of 40 according to Campbell's Anger Flow Chart. Others may name it something else. Whatever one may call it, it is the fourth emotional step away from being happy

CHAPTER FIVE

MAD!

The emotion of being mad is not something to laugh about. However, sometimes after the explosion of being mad and we step back and take a look at our actions we will find some humor. However, I think we might be able to enjoy a humorous life without the experiences that madness brings.

In 1952 William Gaines launched as a comic book titled "Mad." It later became a magazine. While MAD has been accepted as a "humor" magazine there is no humor in dealing with a mad person.

A person that is mad is a person that is experiencing mixed mania. They may feel agitated, angry, irritable, and depressed all at once. Because it combines a high activity level with depression, mixed mania poses a particular danger of suicide or self-injury. So at this step in our emotional anger flow chart we are introduced to the possibility of self destruction. For a person to come to the level of self-destruction and the desire to do physical harm to others there must be enough energy stored up that will explode and cause harm.

At this level of emotions we must teach ourselves to check and evaluate our feelings. What are we doing? What are we saying? It was Ambrose Bierce that said, "Speak when you are mad and you will make the best speech you will ever regret."

What are some of the "best speeches" that you have regretted?

1. _____
   _____

2. _____
   _____

3. _____
   _____

Agitated depression is a major depressive disorder with restlessness and motor excitement. Agitated depression was once called melancholia agitation. It is now also known as mixed mania. Everybody feels sad once in a while. Depression, on the other hand, is a complex condition characterized by profound sadness, feelings of worthlessness, and a loss of interest in social activities. About 15 million people in America suffer with agitated depression.

Being mad is a mood change and if not controlled or identified may lead to other full blown mood disorders. This may lead to one of many disorders or may become what is called a mixed episode and is identified as 296.0 diagnosed by the DSM-IV. The DSM-IV is the "Bible" of the counseling practice and the American Psychiatric Association.

If this behavior is not checked and treated it is possible to lead into other major depression and bi-polar disorders. Depression and stress disorders are building blocks that lead to major disorders including schizophrenia and social disorders. Therefore, it is imperative that prolonged anger be treated. The non-clinician fails to realize that there are over 100 symptoms of anxiety. The leading symptoms for being anxious starts with the feeling of being upset, miffed, frustrated, mad and anger and is most often over looked.

Because each person has a unique chemical makeup, the type, number, intensity, and frequency of anxiety symptoms will vary from person to person. One person may have all the anxiety symptoms and have great severity while another person may have just one mild anxiety symptoms and it will go unnoticed.

Are you able to look in the mirror that does not lie and list the symptoms of the anxiety in your life?

1. _____

2. _____

3. _____

Some major emotional and mood symptoms of anxiety are noticeable in the behavior of the individual in the following examples. When you appear to always be angry and have a lack of being patient.

Your dramatic mood swings and emotional flipping is a good sign of a suffering from anxiety disorder. We justify this negative behavior by offering the excuse that we are "just that way." And therefore, the family question for the day is "what kind of mood are you in today?"

List the mood you are currently in today.

1. _____

2. _____

3. _____

The following emotional feelings that we may have at any time of the day or at any time in our life may cause us to feel down in the dumps. We may just feel like crying all day for no reason.

Have you experienced episodes of crying for no reason? Please describe.

1. _____

2. _____

3. _____

Others may tell us that we are on edge and grouchy but we deny having those emotions. Matter of fact, our household members may feel that everything in the house is scary and frightening. You both may feel like you're walking on egg shells. List what it is that causes you to walk on egg shells.

1. _____

2. _____

3. _____

Other people are able to notice and tell you when you are not feeling like yourself. There is detachment from loved ones and you become emotionally numbed and frighten. Can you list some of the times that you have not felt like yourself?

1. _____
2. _____
3. _____

In a discussion with those who value your relationship and are willing to offer help, you considered them as "sticking their nose in your business," and an argument starts.

When was the last time that someone "got in your business" and how did you feel?"

1. _____
2. _____
3. _____

These arguments will again bring your emotional feelings all over again. You might notice yourself that you have no feelings about things or other people like you used to. You may feel like things are unreal or dreamlike. There is always an underlying anxiety, apprehension and fear. Feeling like you are under pressure all the time becomes a normal life-style.

Can you list the things that you feel you are under pressure about?

1. _____
2. _____

3. _____
_____

We continue in an attempt to have normal relationships but there are always problems. Please note, being anxious and living in a household where anxiety is tolerated is not normal. Do you have any of these emotional and mood symptoms?

If so, list your mood swings and your emotions.

1. _____
_____
2. _____
_____
3. _____
_____

As we allow our emotional feelings to grow and as we continue to feed them our body begins to change. For an example, when we are mad our face displays a frown. We all know that it takes more muscles and energy to frown than to smile. Maybe it is no wonder that we become exhausted. I know after a heated discussion I personally become overly tired. This takes it's told on the body.

Can you list some of the changes in your body that you have notice after getting mad?

1. _____
_____
2. _____
_____
3. _____
_____

The longer our emotions are stuffed the more stressed we become. The more stressed we have the higher our blood pressure. I once had a doctor tell me that my heart disease or a stroke will not kill me. However, he said, that stress and personal anxiety is capable of killing me. He suggested that I eliminate my anxiety and stressors. Now he did not write a prescription but he made a memorial impression on my mind. I left there and began to identify what it was that caused me to become stressed and to have more than my share of anxiety.

Can you list some of your stressors?

1. _____
   _____
2. _____
   _____
3. _____
   _____

So I asked a professional counselor from where is my anger coming? He told me I should know because I wrote the book! Yes we all write our own personal book. No one but us is able to tell where our anger and madness comes from. We may need to dig awhile but we are able to find it. Just keep on digging!

As our body aches, joints stiffens, and immobility sets in, we place band aids by taking pain medications. The deep rooted causes of being mad are never identified. Just give me another pill!

Our body temperature and blood pressure never goes down. Soon chest pains begin to give us problems as the heart is in overdrive. Our digestive system becomes choked and chronic fatigue overcomes our past active lifestyle. Some become obese. Relaxation is a thing of the past. Now our whole body is internally working over time. We are showing signs of aging. Our chest falls to our stomach, our teeth and hair fall out and old age sets in. It is a wonder if we live to retirement. Because of our emotional anger that is not treated our heart pounds and feels like it is beating too hard. We are too busy to realize that if our heart pounds and feels like it's beating too hard it probably is! Hello! Do you know what I am talking about?

If so, list the things that cause your heart to beat out of control.

1. _____
   _____
2. _____
   _____
3. _____
   _____

No wonder our neck, back, and shoulder are in pain as we have tightness and no energy.

List where your pain is located and how sever it is.

1. _____
   _____
2. _____
   _____
3. _____
   _____

Have you ever experienced headaches? Of course, we all have. But how long and how severe are they? Do you have shooting pains, stabbing pains in the face or head? Have you ever had your rib or rib cage draw tight, pressure or feeling like a tight band around the rib cage? These physical pains are often left over tension and stressors from our emotional feelings of being upset, miffed, frustrated, and being mad. If we could put a stop to being so mad we might feel better. Have you ever noticed how much better you feel when you do something good to someone? And how awful you feel when you emotionally stab someone in the back? List some times when you did something good for someone and how if felt?

1. _____
   _____
2. _____
   _____
3. _____
   _____

All of the negative emotions that have been stored up over the years are starting to become too much for us to handle. Some people will question, what is our purpose for living? Why have I made so many mistakes in my life? Is there any happiness anywhere? We begin to think that we are falling apart. The madder we get the more the stress levels increase and the less happy we are in our life.

How do you think you can change some of these feelings?

1. _____
   _____

2. _____

3. _____

Can you list some of the feelings of depression that you have when you become mad?

1. _____

2. _____

3. _____

Can you list how your physical pain increases as you become madder?

1. _____

2. _____

3. _____

Can you describe how deeper your "iceberg" is becoming and can you list some of your "stuff?"

1. _____

2. _____

3. _____

Do you think you could bring yourself to accept that in your Creator's eyes you are created to perfection in His will? Created in His image and as I have been told and as I have told others He doesn't make any junk! So stop driving yourself mad with endless ways to improve, and just accept the glory of your being as you are.

Have you ever thought or said, "That person is really mad?" only to realize that you know that person very well. Who? Me!

Being mad places a person on the score of 50 according to Campbell's Anger Flow Chart. Others may name it something else. Whatever one may call it, it is the fifth emotional step away from being happy

CHAPTER SIX

ANGRY!

Now that you are hurting both emotionally and physically and are mad our next building block is anger. These all, if not identified and placed in check will continue to build until we lose it and end up in the hospital. Most of the time we make statements like, "You make me so mad!" In reality no one makes anyone do anything. We always have a choice not to do anything anytime anywhere! It may kill us and someone else may kill us but in reality we chose to make that decision to do whatever it is that we tell ourselves first and then all others that we were made to do. And if we can't find anyone or anything to blame we will simply state the Devil made me do it. So we never take responsibility for our own action. What a shame!

In these situations we lie to ourselves and again will play the blame game and blame anything or person but ourselves. One of the many elements that contribute to our state of well being is depression. As we become more disappointed with ourselves due to our own failures we become deeper in the state of depression. So it is real easy to get a headache as it is to become one! No wonder after years of failing to place in check our emotions and our physical reactions we become sick. We do in fact make ourselves sick. I have even stated that "I have made myself sick!" You have too?

List some of the times that you have made yourself sick.

1. _____
   _____

2. _____
   _____

3. _____
   _____

I was told once that depression occurs when we have been strong too long! This usually is done solo. We are the only one that is still holding on. There are two results when this happens: One, we get burned out and feel like a failure. Or two, we share with someone that understands and will stick with us like snowflakes. Snowflakes are one of nature's fragile things, but just look what they can do when they stick together! Keep in mind that the total weather setting must be just right. Too often we attempt to get others to see our view and stick with us when it is too hot or cold for them to stick around.

There are always consequences after anger leaves. The consequences of our anger cause many problems. While it is great advice to stop and think not many, are in control of their emotions and physical reaction to think. Instead we often go from happy to anger without the lack of reason, acting foolish, rash, or unwisely. In other words, we can go from 0 to 60 in a split second.

My guess is that a split second is one half of a second. If that be true, then if we respond from being happy to being angry in a split second we become angry at 1800 miles per hour or mach 3. No wonder there are explosions. I know people that can and will become angry in a blink of the eye. I believe I have been guilty of doing this very thing. How about you?

Can you list some of the experiences that you have had in getting angry in a split second?

1. _____
   _____
2. _____
   _____
3. _____
   _____

How do we do that? I think we do it by practicing. We become good at this action or reactions. Matter of fact, some are able to go much faster. They are able and will often go from happy to out of control in a split second. I think that is about the speed of light!

Mach 3 speed by a person is really insane. We might think that a person has instantly missed so much in life. If this behavior continues over a period of time we might say they are suffering from being mentally disturbed.

Most anger issues are when a person is already upset, miffed, frustrated, afraid and mad mixed with some degree of fear. Anger is displayed by frantic behavior showing or resulting from lack of reason; foolish, rash, unwise, distracted and distraught action.

Can you list some of the times and reasons that you have been afraid and mad?

1. _____
   _____

2. _____
   _____

3. _____
   _____

In feeding our mad emotions we become angry. Mad and angry go together like dirt and mud. Anger is madness mixed with tears and mud is dirt ~~with~~ mixed with the same wet tears. We now are flirting with danger. Danger is when a person is angry and begins to "lose it.' If this is not stopped in its track we will move on to a very dangerous state of being out of control. Therefore, we must learn that being mad is one tear drop from anger and anger is just one letter away from danger.

Can you list some dangerous actions or reactions as the result of you being angry?

1. _____
   _____

2. _____
   _____

3. _____
   _____

A few years ago, it was popular to say "the Devil made me do it." I have wondered, if the Devil made you do it, then the "D" in danger" must come from the Devil himself. That is scary. Anger becomes to the level of being dangerous as we allow anger to live with us. Could it be that for most of us we did not know how close the Devil is to us? That is, we eat with anger, we sleep with anger, we live with anger and anger consumes our emotions. We may become angry all the time. How much negative control do we give when angry?

At the danger point our emotions of anger give energy to fight. It is easy to fight anyone over anything when we are under the influence of anger. We think the world is all against us. The only way we know to handle the world caving in on us is to fight back. We are now also moving deeper into depression. Depression and anger runs together as the deeper the anger the deeper the depression. Have you ever seen anyone that is angry and happy? Have you seen anyone that is depressed and happy? Of course not! As this is a negative emotion.

So what is anger? Can you describe what you think anger is?

1. _____
_____
2. _____
_____
3. _____
_____

Anger is a strong emotion of displeasure caused by some type of grievance that is either real or perceived to be real by a person. The cognitive behavior theory attributes anger to several factors such as past experiences, behavior learned from others, genetic predispositions, and a lack of problem-solving ability. To put it more simply, anger is caused by a combination of two factors: an irrational perception of reality ("It has to be done my way") and a low frustration point ("It's my way or no way").

Anger is an internal reaction that is perceived to have an external cause. Angry people almost always blame their reactions on some person or event, but rarely do they realize that the reason they are angry is because of their irrational perception of their world. Angry people have a certain perception and expectation of the world that they live in. When that reality does not meet their expectation then they become angry.

Can you list some of the times that expectations did not meet your requirements?

1. _____
_____

2. _____
   _____
3. _____
   _____

It is important to understand that not all anger is unhealthy. Anger is one of our most primitive defense mechanisms that protects and motivates us from being dominated or manipulated by others. It gives us the added strength, courage, and motivation needed to combat injustice done against us or to others that we love. However, if anger is left uncontrolled and free to take over the mind and body at any time and at will, then anger may become destructive. Therefore, it appears that one may be suffering from chronic anger issues.

Why do we need to control our anger? Can you list some reason why we would need to control our anger?

1. _____
   _____
2. _____
   _____
3. _____
   _____

Just like a person who is under the control of any substance, a person under the influence of anger cannot rationalize, comprehend, or make good decisions because anger distorts logical reasoning into blind emotion. Have you ever said or thought that you were hit from the blind side of life? I have often times said, "I never saw that coming!"

Have you ever experienced being blindsided?

1. _____
   _____
2. _____
   _____
3. _____
   _____

This is true with people with a clear mind. All of our emotions will become more highly amplified when the person is using drugs or alcohol. Any type of substance use including prescription medication will alter our emotional responses. In other words, substances add fuel to the fire.

A person becomes unable to think clearly and their emotions take control of their actions. Physiologically speaking, anger enacts the fight or flight response in our brain, which increases our blood pressure and releases adrenaline into our bloodstream, thereby increasing our strength and pain threshold.

Anger makes us think of only two things: (1) defend, or (2) attack. Neither of these options facilitates a good negotiation.

Can you list some of the times that you have become defensive?

1. _____
_____
2. _____
_____
3. _____
_____

Can you list some of the times that you have gone on the attack?

1. _____
_____
2. _____
_____
3. _____
_____

A natural response to pain or being hurt is anger. We might say it is part of the instinctive animal nature of any being. We perceive danger with being hurt, the fight mechanism of anger helps to ensure our protection. However our fight mechanism does not necessarily operate on rationality. It operates on our assumptions and beliefs.

We often aren't aware of how our beliefs operate and how they create our emotions so they may seem hidden. However, these beliefs aren't really hidden. It's that we haven't been looking for them. Most often we accept our first level of assumption and our first thoughts about things without reflecting any deeper.

A key to anger prevention is to identify the false beliefs at the root of your emotions. Beliefs are the elemental structure in the mind that causes us to generate certain thoughts and interpretations about things. False beliefs, coupled with other factors like, point of view, combine to create destructive emotional reactions.

Two major ingredients to a person's anger are fear, and a perception of being mistreated or abused. Therefore anger may lack compassion and sympathy. When the abuse or fear is in the imagination of the person, anger is still an emotional reaction. The causes of anger aren't seen consequently and this makes anger a natural fight or flight survival response to a real threat of abuse.

Can you list some of the times your anger was because of fear?

1. _____
2. _____
3. _____

Can you list some of the times your anger was because of mistreatment or abuse?

1. _____
2. _____
3. _____

I have never as of yet seen anyone that is happily angry. I have never seen anyone that was suffering either or both emotional or physical pain and are extremely satisfied and happy. It then becomes difficult at times for us to get on with our life.

Moving on with our life is hard to do when our body has a tingling sensation and our hand shake. Our head hurts as it just pounding! For couples, we become sexually dysfunctional and uninterested with unresolved madness and anger. If for some reason you don't believe me just make your mate angry and see for yourself.

Can you list how often this occurs in your relationship?

1. _____
2. _____
3. _____

The building blocks continue to stack up. From chapter one, we learned that being upset was our first step toward anger. Then as we give food to being upset we become a little miffed. No harm! Oh but is there? Then we become frustrated. We are more upset and unable to remember were we left our car keys. We forgot what we were attempting to talk about and we now know that we are starting to hurt. "I have a headache" is usually the first physical indication of our pain. So we begin with talking [taking] an aspirin. How often do you take aspirin or other medications for headaches?

1. _taking_____
2. _____
3. _____

Now the fear factor is increased and we become worried. We become worried about most everything in our life. We begin to second guess ourselves. As the building blocks continue to be laid our emotions become irritated. Our iceberg grows and grows. It gets bigger and bigger. Our stuff is stuffed! After all we are adults and we can handle it. Me of all people, I do not need professional help. So I will just talk to a friend. Talking to a friend is free and it makes me feel good. But in reality talking to a friend never solves your deep rooted and decades of stuffing your inward hurt never got fixed. You get what you paid for, nothing!

Can you list some of the times that you have called your friend and discussed your problems?

    1. _____
       _____

    2. _____
       _____

    3. _____
       _____

If you feel like you need to talk to a friend or someone you might want to call a professional counselor and start your healing process.

With our new found irritations comes a good dose of madness. And we know that being mad is only one step away from being angry. Full blown anger!

What makes you have full blown anger?

    1. _____
       _____

    2. _____
       _____

    3. _____
       _____

Now it is easier for us to feel the stress in our life. Easier for us to feel the chest pain and discomfort that we justify as indigestion. If you find it hard to breath with chest pains and tingles in the left armpit and going down your left arm please call 911 and get medical help before you die! Note that women have much different symptoms as do men. Women, if you even think for one moment that you are experiencing heart related pain get help quickly! If anyone finds it hard to breath, feeling smothered, shortness of breath, and your heart is beating hard, too fast, flutter or maybe just a tickle in the chest that makes you cough I would encourage to see your doctor.

Describe how your chest pain come and go.

    1. _____
       _____

2. _____
   _____

3. _____
   _____

Being angry may cause many symptoms both emotional and physically.

Can you list some of the symptoms that you have emotionally as the result of your anger?

1. _____
   _____

2. _____
   _____

3. _____
   _____

Can you list some of the symptoms that you have physically as the result of your anger?

1. _____
   _____

2. _____
   _____

3. _____
   _____

Have you ever thought or said, "That person is really angry?" only to realize that you know that person very well. Who? Me!

The anger emotion places a person on the score of 60 and according to Campbell's Anger Flow Chart you are living in the "danger zone." In this area of emotion someone may get hurt or hurt themselves. You may call it something else. Whatever you may call it, it is the sixth emotional step away from being happy.

CHAPTER SEVEN

FIGHT!

After flying off the handle, the last thing you want to hear is "Police!" By flying off the handle and to "lose it" for awhile offend times leads to a very heated discussion and a fight! What does it mean to you?

Can you list some of the times when you know that you flew off the handle at someone or something?

1. _____
   _____

2. _____
   _____

3. _____
   _____

The following is my summarization of a report by Dan Wetzel who is a Yahoo Sports' national columnist. The story has been told nationally on both the radio and television sport shows. This story describes the emotions of anger and the potential of it getting out of hand and moving on to a locker room fight. However, due to reasoning, clear thinking and subconscious identification of their emotional anger flow the two quarterbacks were able to put a stop to their altercation, hug each other and walk out as real Steelers.

One of the most talked about potential fight in football history has been between the past quarterback of the Pittsburgh Steelers Terry Bradshaw and the present QB Ben Roethlisberger. A face-to-face show down between the two men would probably result in a blow by blow fight in the locker room!

Each man is known by thousands of fans for publicly expressing their anger with each other. Likewise they have thousands of fans that would argue and fight for them. Both men are and have been record setting quarterbacks and are successful on and off the field. Mutually these two have emotionally allowed a problem, events, and circumstances move them from being upset, miffed, frustrated, mad and angry. They have fed their emotions and allowed their relationship to grow into the state of being toxic.

When a relationship becomes toxic and one or the other feel they are backed into a corner our human defense will surface and either a verbal fight occurs or possibly physical blows may result. It doesn't matter who you are or what you have and what records you may hold, we all are alike. Remember that anger is just one letter from danger.

It is public knowledge that last year, Ben was accused of sexually assaulting a twenty year old college student in Georgia. When the news broke, Terry began dogging him in his interviews and made the comment that if the original owner, Art Rooney, was still alive Ben would have been ran out of town.

It has been reported in the public news that Roethlisberger had said that he thought Terry spoke a little too soon, before he knew all the facts. This is what we call a perception of being mistreated. Beliefs are the elemental structure in the mind that causes us to generate certain thoughts and interpretations about things. False beliefs, coupled with other factors like, point of view, combine to create destructive emotional reactions. Terry's and Ben's destructive emotional reactions to each other could have exploded into a possible locker room fight.

Have you ever felt that someone has some false beliefs about you or an event in your life and are making statements that hurt you and are upsetting to you?

1. _____

2. _____

3. _____

Have you felt like Ben in this situation? After all, Ben's incident led to no legal charges. However there was a four game NFL suspension. Nevertheless, criticism rained down on him.

Bradshaw's repeated comments may have stung the most. As he said that he has two daughters and anybody that is mistreating women doesn't sit well with him! He admitted that he did not know all of the facts. He said he may have rushed to judgment too quickly. But it was because it was the second time Ben was accused of sexual assault in 2008. He admitted that influenced his hostility.

Have you ever experienced how Terry feels and where he is coming from too?

1. _____
2. _____
3. _____

According to Bradshaw, this is what Roethlisberger has formed and he must repair. He may not have been charged with a crime, but his actions were crude and repulsive. It mired his reputation as a low-life who just happened to be blessed with a strong arm.

Ben continues to tell people he is a changed man.

The two hadn't spoken in person since the incident. According to Bradshaw, Roethlisberger refused to shake his hand at Steelers training camp last summer, a scene Bradshaw described as "icy cold." Their only interaction was a brief, shallow interview during a Pro Bowl telecast.

"He doesn't like me, and I'm learning not to like him," Bradshaw said last offseason. Is there someone that doesn't like you and you are learning not to like them?

Would you dare list them and the circumstances?

1. _____
2. _____
3. _____

Bradshaw wanted a sit-down interview and no one knew what Roethlisberger would do. Ben may have walked away or screamed in Bradshaw's face. Who knows he may slug someone! "We weren't sure he would sit down with me," Bradshaw said. "Everyone was nervous."

The sports crew was on edge. Well, everyone except for Bradshaw, who still maintains his cool. The co-host Howie Long said, "Terry was calming me down."

Bradshaw was going to try to defuse the entire situation. Approaching Roethlisberger immediately, "Terry wanted to talk to me," he said "He pulled me aside inside the locker room!"

Have you ever attempted to defuse a disagreement or an argument?

1. _____
_____

2. _____
_____

3. _____
_____

The locker room was set up for an interview but in order to clear the air, Bradshaw cleared the place out. Cameramen, sound technicians, producers and everyone else was told to leave. Someone had come up with the idea that if Roethlisberger was willing to speak to Bradshaw at all, they should first do it alone, man-to-man, eye-to-eye, Steeler-to-Steeler. If peace could be reached, then they'd turn on the cameras.

"Take everyone else out of the room, let the two of us sit down and have a talk," Bradshaw said. "And if you want to get it off your chest, get it off." They went back and forth for a few minutes.

Bradshaw said, the bad blood had dated back to Bradshaw criticizing Roethlisberger for getting in a 2006 motorcycle accident. Some in the Roethlisberger camp believed Bradshaw was unduly harsh on Roethlisberger because he feared his record of four Super Bowl championships was in jeopardy.

Then came that drunken night in Georgia that left Bradshaw convinced he was right all along.

Roethlisberger didn't provide any new facts about the case, according to Bradshaw. They both aired their various points of view. Roethlisberger was seeking fairness, perspective and understanding.

He was asking for a second chance. He kept addressing his elder as "Sir" and "Mr. Bradshaw."

Roethlisberger was seeking nothing more than you or I would have hoped for: fairness, perspective and understanding.

Have you ever been where Ben was at in this "peace making" conference?

1. _____
2. _____
3. _____

Have you ever been where Terry was at his approach to making resolution with Ben?

1. _____
2. _____
3. _____

Bradshaw, meanwhile, wanted Roethlisberger to know he wasn't jealous and he wanted him to break all his records. He then defended his role as tell-it-like-it-is television analyst. If I feel it's necessary to say I'm sorry, 'I'm sorry,' " Bradshaw said. "But basically I'm just doing my job. I don't want to hurt anybody. I'm just in an unfortunate business where if you ask me a question I have to answer it honestly and if I don't answer it truthfully then I'm not respected."

Do you remember how I talked about being truthful in the beginning? Life requires that we are truthful with ourselves and truthful with others. Remember that the mirror doesn't lie?

What you see is what you get. What are you seeing now in your mirror?

1. _____

2. _____

3. _____

According to Bradshaw, Roethlisberger was both humble about his failures and hopeful about his future. There are many people who don't believe the sincerity of either of those things and, at one point Bradshaw was probably the chief among them. Somewhere in that converted locker room, he changed his mind.

Have you ever changed your mind about someone before?

1. _____

2. _____

3. _____

"Of course people say, 'Oh, it's not real,'" Bradshaw said. "I think it's totally real." Time will tell if what Roethlisberger says he understands. "Just keep plugging away," he said of proving himself to the public. Stay out of trouble and do the right thing and perhaps, one day, the focus on him won't be about the mistakes he's made. It's up to the people though. He isn't owed forgiveness.

If fans seek signs of progress, of maturity, then maybe this is a small one. Last summer Ben Roethlisberger wouldn't shake Terry Bradshaw's hand, too much anger getting in the way of reconciliation. Yet, the two Steelers legends ended their discussion with a hug.

Have you ever ended a harsh relationship with a hand shake or better yet a great hug? If so, list some.

1. _____

2. _____

3. _____

We have two great examples of anger management between two high profile individuals that the world of football and others are watching. I want to thank them both for their maturity level and their examples to all of us and our children. We must remember that hero's are human and they make mistakes and need our help often a second chance.

Have you ever needed a second chance in life?

1. _____
2. _____
3. _____

"We just both came to the conclusion that we're Steelers, we're part of that family," Bradshaw said. "And I encouraged him that yesterday is yesterday and that I have his back and I support him 100 percent. "But if he screws up again ... I'll do it again."

Most of our fighting over being angry and hurt is with others that we respect and love. If they didn't care and if we didn't care we might just move on. But when our emotions and love is involved we get hurt. It's the hurt and pain that we need to have fixed. Most of the time to words "I'm sorry" and a hug is all that is needed to fix it!

Have you ever been the one that needs to say, "I'm sorry?"

1. _____
2. _____
3. _____

Most of fighting is verbal, face to face or on the phone and by the mail. I had almost failed to realize that there are some people who chose to do their fighting by texting and email. Our new found e-behavior is a growing concern. I know that may sound strange but when someone's sending you relentlessly demanding e-mails and text messages, it can be easy to pick up that tone and snap back. Is it better for you to do your fighting by e-behavior?

56   Who? Me! Angry?

Can you list some of your e-mail heated verbal fights lately?

1. _____
   _____
2. _____
   _____
3. _____
   _____

Fighting brings fear. And fear brings tons of other actions and reactions. These are both emotional and physical. Some of our fears have no basis. They are what we think things are instead of how they really are in real life. However, our fear will give us a big dose of anxiety.

We become afraid of what people think about us. We have fear of losing control of our domain. We become filled with a constant feeling of being overwhelmed. We place limits on ourselves as we are afraid of making mistakes or making a fool of ourselves. to others.

Can you list some of your fears that are causing you to be overwhelmed?

1. _____
   _____
2. _____
   _____
3. _____
   _____

We develop a hysterical fear about irrational things, objects, circumstances or situations that have not happened and probably will not occur. We might even have a heightened self awareness of self-consciousness over the smallest of things or events.

Fighting is a result of feeling trapped. Fighting may be the result of an underlying fear, apprehension or anxieties that we are dealing with and is problematic. You often feel you are carrying the world on your shoulders and there is no way out but to come out fighting.

What are some of the weights that are on your shoulders?

1. _____
   _____

2. _____
   _____
3. _____
   _____

What someone has told you or what you think others are saying about you keeps replaying over and over again in your mind. You are stuck in these thoughts and mental images or concepts. You become numb. You feel like you are under pressure all the time.

Have you ever had these feelings before?

1. _____
   _____
2. _____
   _____
3. _____
   _____

Physically we may have stomach problems like constipation or diarrhea. We have difficulty swallowing and making certain sounds, talking or pronouncing certain letters. We might even begin to slur our speech. And the thought of eating make you nauseous. These are all signs of anxiety, or we might call it stress.

Have you had these systems before? *SYMPTOMS*

1. _____
   _____
2. _____
   _____
3. _____
   _____

There are many sources for anger that leads to fighting. One is our internal sources. Our internal sources of anger come from our irrational perceptions of reality. Most psychologists agree and have identified some of the following as internal sources that contribute to anger and our need to fight.

Some who reason emotionally misinterpret normal events and things that other people see as being directly threatening to their needs and goals. People who use emotional reasoning tend to become irritated at something innocent that other people tell them because they perceive it as an attack on themselves. Emotional reasoning can lead to dysfunctional anger in the long run.

Do you use any emotional reasoning that irritates you with other people? If so, please list them.

1. _____
2. _____
3. _____

All of us at some point have experienced a time where our tolerance for frustration was low. Often stress-related anxiety lowers our tolerance for frustration and we begin to perceive normal things as threats to our well-being or threats to our ego.

Have you ever perceived normal things as threats to your well-being? If so, please list them.

1. _____
2. _____
3. _____

Some people make demands and they see things as how they should be and not as they really are. This lowers their frustration tolerance because people who have unreasonable expectations expect others to act a certain way, or for uncontrollable events to behave in a predictable manner. When these things do not go their way, then anger, frustration, and eventually depression will set in.

Can you list some of the times that this has happened to you?

1. _____

2. _____
   _____
3. _____
   _____

People watching or people-rating are an anger-causing type of thinking where the person applies a derogatory label on someone else. By rating them with any type of insulting names dehumanizes them and makes it easier for them to become angry at the person.

Have you ever rated others and used derogatory labels? If so, can you list them?

1. _____
   _____
2. _____
   _____
3. _____
   _____

These actions may result in deep depression in addition to many other things such as fighting. The emotions and fears both real and unreal may cause chronic illness, difficulty in our relationships. Many people have financial problems and many unwelcome changes in their life patterns that are triggered by a depressive episode. Have you ever thought or said, "That person is really ready to fight!" Only to realize that you know that person very well! Who? Me!

The emotion of fighting places a person on the score of 70 and you are in the danger zone, according to Campbell's Anger Flow Chart. Other may name it something else. Whatever one may call it, it is the eighth emotional step away from being happy. I feel I must issue a warning notice as when someone is in a rage it may be time to call for professional help. It may be time to call 911. People in a rage are capable of harming themselves as well as others.

CHAPTER EIGHT

RAGE!

It was Marcus Antonius that said, "Consider how much more you often suffer from your anger and grief, than from those very things for which you are angry and grieved." A lot of the time we have difficulties falling asleep or once asleep staying asleep.

Rage is a deeply rooted emotion that may keep you awake all night. Rage feeds our anger and our anger will feed our rage. It is a merry go round that has no stopping on its own. Something or someone must intervene. Once the flight [RAGE] is over there appears to be a time of what happened and how did I get here?

Have you ever experienced one or both of these moments?

1. _____

2. _____

3. _____

Rage is most often understood as uncontrolled anger, usually of brief duration. It is driven by hostility. Hostility is a motivating force, a conscious or unconscious impulse, tendency, intent or reactions aimed at injuring or destroying and usually accompanied by the feeling or emotions of anger.

Can you list some of the times that your rage has gotten out of control?

1. _____

2. _____
   _____
3. _____
   _____ OR

Rage has obvious, behavioral expressions, whereas hostility involves a strong element of calculation and control. Rage brings hostility but hostility does not bring rage. Some related concepts that are important in the understand of rage and hostility are anger, as a feeling, imagined injury, and cruelty, the actual behavior of inflicting suffering on another, usually without just cause of the expression of mercy. The aggression of rage is understood as the energetic pursuit of desire to dominate and when used positively it refers to vigorous initiative in the pursuit of one's goals.

Can you list some of the events in your life in which rage has taken control?

1. _____
   _____
2. _____
   _____
3. _____
   _____

It is less well known about rage than about anxiety that its major function is a signaling one. When rage is present, the self is threatened. Whatever issue or circumstance triggered the rage has, by the time rage is felt, become secondary to dealing with the security needs of the person or persons exhibiting it.

Can you list some of the issues that trigger rage within yourself?

1. _____
   _____
2. _____
   _____
3. _____
   _____

A secondary significance to rage is its intensity, its association with self-righteousness, and its function of extrication person from apathetic dullness. Stated simply, we often feel better being angry than depressed, particularly if we can convince ourselves that the rage we feel is justified. Thus rage may be unconsciously chosen as an alternative to painful self-doubt and the depression that often accompanies it.

Can you list a few times that you have felt that it better to be angry than to be depressed?

1. _____
2. _____
3. _____

In contrast to rage, which is too physically exhausting to last for long periods of time, hostility is colder and more calculating and may be maintained indefinitely. Its significance lies in its having captured the person's overall view of the world and therefore, his or her perception of particular situations so that rational and constructive actions, untrained by hostility, are precluded.

The destructions of rage lie in the feeling of oneself rather than in responding to an external stimulus. Many of the negative things that persons have been inappropriately told about anger may be appropriately said about rage. Whereas it can be a constructive experience to find ways of expressing anger, this is not the case with rage. The source of rage is not an issue or circumstance but the self's sense of importance; therefore discovering the ability to control our rage contributes more to the self's security than anything resembling uncontrolled expression.

Can you list some of your efforts to control your rage?

1. _____
2. _____

64 Who? Me! Angry?

3. _____
   _____

The appropriate response to one's own rage is an attempt through self-reflecting and for counseling and supervision to understand its sources and to develop enough security in significant relationships so that it becomes unnecessary. The appropriate response to rage is an understanding that the rage or hostility probably results more from a threat to you than to the specific circumstance which triggered it.

Can you list some of the attempts through your own self-reflecting that has helped you?

1. _____
   _____
2. _____
   _____
3. _____
   _____

Some of the symptoms of rage are insomnia and waking up ill in the middle of the night, or waking up in a panic attack and in need of a Xanax. This is of course only a band-aid as it does not get to the bottom of the issues. As you wake up in the morning you feel worse than the morning before. Alprazolam medications are Xanax's that is given for the treatment of anxiety and panic disorders.

It may be a good time to list all of the medications that you are taking and for what purpose you take it?

1. _____
   _____
2. _____
   _____
3. _____
   _____
4. _____
   _____
5. _____
   _____

6. _____
   _____

7. _____
   _____

8. _____
   _____

9. _____
   _____

10. _____
    _____

You noticed I have given a list of ten places for med's because some people do take ten or more different pills daily. Then we shake our heads and wonder how someone like Michael Jackson can take a "Cocktail" of medications. I am surprised at how many pills the doctors have their clients taking daily.

Can you now look in your mirror being honest with yourself ask if you are taking a "Cocktail" of pills?

_____ Yes

_____ No

A cocktail is a mixture of sustains. We normally think of a drink at a bar scene.

But with medication it is very easy to become use to taking more than one or two pills. As we grow older we become more dependent on different medications for all of the elements that we think we are developing. So therefore, it is too easy for the aged to begin to take a "Cocktail" of medications.

I know you have all the right answers after all it was your doctor that told you that you needed them. Right? Well, that is true to a point. Was it not you that first told your doctor that you needed something for some "relief?" So what do you think your doctor should have done with you? Let's see, he or she could have said you will get better in a day or two and sent you home. Or they could have asked more questions and spent hours with you that none of them have and probably would have told you to reduce your stress and you will feel better! But later, that is without the magical "pill" for the "band-aid."

66   Who? Me! Angry?

And we never do much to help ourselves and take action to reduce our stress. All the "stuff" that keeps us upset!

If they were good doctors they already know that you are stressed. Your body tells on you. Keep looking in your mirror and you will see what I am talking about. As you are looking in your mirror can you see things that your face tells that you are stressed about and if so arre [are] you able to list them?

1. _____
_____
2. _____
_____
3. _____
_____HAVE-A-HEART-TO-HEART_____

Now can you identify the medication that your doctor has prescribed for you to take for these medical conditions? Under no circumstances should anyone ever haveaheart-to-heart discussion with your doctors. You should have a full understanding of the medications that you are currently taking and to understand why you are taking them..

Rage brings physical symptoms such as muscle twinges, worry, tingles, gagging and tightness. Anxiety sets in and chest pain occurs. Heart beat problems occurs and we develop pain in the legs and other joints

Can you list where your pain is located?

1. _____
_____
2. _____
_____
3. _____
_____

Have you ever thought or said, "That person is really in a rage" only to realize that you know that person very well. Who? Me! Angry?

While our emotions play havoc with us our physical condition begins to break down. We experience heart attacks, heart disease, and strokes. We experience serious undetected illnesses such as cancer and possibly losing it!

Have you ever felt like this before?

1. _____

2. _____

3. _____

Given the parameters of a negotiating situation, we can narrow these factors down to four general sources.

First of all: Someone makes personal attack against you or someone that you love such as a spouse, child, family member or friend. That person attacks you along with the problem in the form of verbal abuse. Now we have the start of a nice verbal fight! We have gone from zero to 60 plus in a split second or quicker and with an explosion.

Can you list any time that you have had this done to you?

1. _____

2. _____

3. _____

Can you now list any time that you have done this to someone else?

1. _____

2. _____

3. _____

Secondly, another example is when someone attacks an idea that you have. Matter-of-fact they just chop down your opinions, ideas, and any options that you may have concerning an idea.

Has anyone done this to you and if so can you list them?

1. _____
2. _____
3. _____

Be honest now, have you ever done that to anyone? If so, list them. This is a very healing exercise.

1. _____
2. _____
3. _____

Thirdly, when a problem arises as someone threatens our needs. The person threatens to take away a basic need of ours if they do not get their way. Usually, it is said in the following manner. "I'll make sure you will never work in this profession again!"

Has anyone ever said something of that nature to you?

1. _____
2. _____
3. _____

Again, I will ask you to be honest and truthful with yourself and list the times that you have made this type of statement to someone yourself.

1. _____
2. _____

3. _____
   _____

Fourthly, it is easy for anyone at anytime to become in a rage. Our tolerance level for getting things done might be lower from time to time. We will be affected by any number of factors in our lives.

Can you identify some of the things that cause your frustrations to be lower from time to time and you fly off in a rage?

1. _____
   _____
2. _____
   _____
3. _____
   _____

The emotion of rage places a person on the score of 80 and you are living in the danger zone according to Campbell's Anger Flow Chart. Others may name it something else. Whatever one may call it, it is the eighth emotional step away from being happy

I feel I must issue a warning notice as when someone is in a rage it may be time to call for professional help. It may be time to call 911. People in a rage are capable of harming themselves as well as others.

CHAPTER NINE

IRRATIONAL!

Emerson stated that, "For every minute you remain angry, you give up sixty seconds of peace of mind." It was Elizabeth Kenny that said, "He who angers you conquers you." How true these statements are!

We have been and are looking for the truth in our relationships. Hopefully we have been looking for the truth in ourselves. Any involvement in a relationship will depend on the truth. It is hard for an individual to look at themselves as being in a relationship with ourselves. In reality, we all are in a personal relationship with ourselves. For some reason most people do not like themselves. Many have told me in counseling sessions that they hate themselves. Or they hate their looks, be it their nose, ears, hair or being too fat. There seems to be something wrong with everyone within our own relationship with ourselves.

What are some of the things that you do not like about you self? *[handwritten: yourself]*

1. _____
2. _____
3. _____

I have had many people laugh at me when I refer to the three personalities that I claim that live within me. They are: "me," "myself" and "I." Those three will argue and disagree with themselves. I may think that "I" should not say something and "myself" will encourage "me" to go ahead and say it. Or it may be any combination of things, actions or words that are running through my mind.

Can you list some of the times, the events or the words that you have experienced this inward battle?

1. _____
   _____

2. _____
   _____

3. _____
   _____

These inward battles add to our stress levels and if not placed in check may cause anxiety. Our anxieties increases, our tolerance for frustration decreases. This becomes a balancing act. When one becomes heavy with anger it is one of many reasons for what we label as domestic disputes. We use to call it family fighting. Regardless of the label it is a negative emotion that causes negative feelings in our relationships. This negative starts from within and acts outwardly to others.

Can you list some of the times that you have become overwhelmed with these negative feelings?

1. _____
   _____

2. _____
   _____

3. _____
   _____

The increase in stress that is not placed in check leads to being anxious. Our muscles will tighten up with negative emotions. Matter of fact, our face will tell on us. Without relief, our head will begin to hurt and we will start having headaches. That's right! Pain! Physical and emotional pain lowers our frustration tolerance. We are so focused on taking care of our survival needs, that we do not have time for anything or anyone.

Can you identify some of your physical pain that you know comes directly from your emotional pain?

1. _____
   _____

2. _____
   _____
3. _____
   _____

Hopefully, you have already listed your medications for your medicinal needs. Some people are able to justify usage in different proportions of "just having a beer or two" or "just a glass of wine." While these "drinks" may be legal and done privately of your own home or in the public, these have an added effect on how the brain processes information it can make a person more irritable or bring forward repressed emotions or memories that can trigger anger.

Can you list some of the times that this has happened to you?

1. _____
   _____
2. _____
   _____
3. _____
   _____

Irritations can also be called "having a bad day." It's the little irritations that add up during the course of the day that lower our tolerance. Therefore, irritations can be like stepping in a puddle, spilling food on your shirt, being late for work or any number of other problems of the day. These all add up to us being irritated and having a bad day..

Can you share some of your "bad day" experiences?

1. _____
   _____
2. _____
   _____
3. _____
   _____

This feels like the world is falling in and we just can't handle anymore. Have you ever felt like that?

Can you list some of the problems that have caused you to have that "world falling" feeling?

1. _____
   _____
2. _____
   _____
3. _____
   _____

Recently, in my hometown newspaper there was an article about a late thirty year old mother. It was reported that she was placed in jail and was facing a criminal homicide charge after she allegedly shot and killed her daughter's boyfriend. This happened after an argument according to the local police department. Now it appears that she became angry, in a rage, willing to fight, and moved on to being irrational. All of this could have been prevented had she had the skills of anger management and stopped! Walked away! Chilled out and this young seventeen year old boy would still be alive! This has become a way of life. This action occurs daily. And we say that we live in a period of history of understanding and forgiveness of one another.

The officers at the scene said they heard several stories about what happened. There are always different stories. Someone once said that if there are ten witnesses there will be ten different stories. So how does the truth ever come out? It is reported that multiple neighbors confirmed that about twenty to twenty-five people, most of whom appeared school age, were fighting. The fight that led to the shooting was connected to a bus stop confrontation that began earlier near the shooting site.

A neighborhood leader reported that at the bus stop there were two girls doing most of the fighting and the confrontation moved down the street. It just grew bigger and bigger. The boy who was shot became involved when he tried to protect a friend. At first he was trying to stop it. That's when he got hit in the head with the golf club. At that point, the fight wasn't just between teenagers. There were some grown-ups that grabbed him and slung him down, then there was a 'pow' and then there was a man down.

Several months ago there was another bus stop shooting involving teenagers. A truck drove by the bus stop and its passengers fired multiple shots but no one was injured. This would appear to be an ongoing event of anger in the neighborhood and between teenagers and adults as well.

Can you list some ways that this shooting could have been prevented?

1. _____

2. _____

3. _____

Another report by the local police department, reported that two brothers. One brother went to jail and the other brother went to the local hospital. One man is charged with attempted first degree murder and aggravated assault after he allegedly shot his brother. Nothing much has changed since Cain killed his brother Abel. Why? Would you not think that after all these years we could learn to control our emotional feelings and the pain that it brings.

Can you list some of the times that you have held harsh feelings and harbored anger within yourself?

1. _____

2. _____

3. _____

My question is when is all of this going to stop? Or is it ever?

It must begin from within each of us. There are physiological signs of anger that our body and emotions give out. We can learn to recognize these signs. By recognizing the physiological signs of anger, we can attune ourselves to know when it is time to take measures to make sure that our level of anger does not move on and get out of control.

Here are some symptoms and signs of anger: unconscious tensing of muscles, especially in the face and neck, teeth grinding, dramatic increase in breathing rate increases dramatically, face turns red face, ears turn purple and veins start to become visible due to increased in blood pressure, face turns pale, sweating, feeling hot or cold, shaking in the hands. Goosebumps with increased heart rate and your adrenaline is released in your system creating a surge of power.

Can you list the times that your emotional feelings have come to the level of anger that has driven you to experience any of the above symptoms and signs?

1. _____
_____
2. _____
_____
3. _____
_____

Do you have a right to be angry? The answer is yes. There is a "but," involved in our anger issues. We all have our own perception and expectation of the world that we live in and when the reality that we live in fails to meet our expectations, and then yes you have the right to be angry. After all, if everyone thought alike, then the world would be a pretty dull place to live. We are going to run into situations that we don't enjoy. We are going to run into people who don't respect our views and ideas. The feeling of anger is totally justified according to our beliefs and so don't repress or deny those feelings.

Having to right to feel angry does not mean that we have the right to lash out in anger by attacking the other person. We can't change the views of other people to conform to our own. Like us, they have their own right to uphold their view of the world. The best thing we can do is to recognize our anger and learn to manage it.

Can you list some of the ways that you have learned to manage your anger?

1. _____
_____
2. _____
_____
3. _____
_____

Some ways to defeat anger would be in how we speak to others. And how we react to other people in both our emotions and physically. To learn to speak the following statements to those who attempt to make us angry could make a difference.

I would encourage you to take one of the following statements per week until they become a part of your speech. I love you! Good thinking! Good for you! Much better! Thanks for helping! Marvelous! Super! What a great idea! That's the way! Nice going! Good thinking! Keep it up! Great try! Way to go! Outstanding! Much better! Thanks for helping! Congratulations! Marvelous! What a great idea! Looking good! I'm impressed! Super work! I'm proud of you! Fabulous! Better than ever! What a champ! Look at you go! Keep on trying! Sensational! How clever! Perfect! There's nobody like you! I knew you could do it! How thoughtful! Exactly right! Great answer! How nice of you! I've got faith in you! Wonderful! Terrific! Have you noticed that these are all positive exclamation statements? And no one will get angry at you for using this speak.

Can you list some people that you would like for them to speak these words to you?

1. _____
_____
2. _____
_____
3. _____
_____

The change in communication might need to begin with us. The person you see in the mirror.

Can you list someone that you need to share the above words with as soon as possible?

1. _____
_____
2. _____
_____
3. _____
_____

Have you ever thought or said, "That person is really irrational?" only to realize that you know the person very well. Who? Me! Irrational!

Being irrational places a person on the score of 90 and you are in the danger zone according to Campbell's Anger Flow Chart. Others may name it something else. Whatever one may call it, it is the ninth emotional step away from being happy. I feel I must issue a warning notice as when someone becomes irrational it may be time to call for professional help. It may be time to call 911.

CHAPTER TEN

OUT OF CONTROL!

I once heard that "Being angry never solves anything!" Anger is a destructive force like fire. It can destroy your home, your business, your career, and your personal relationships. I wouldn't attempt to manage a fire in my house or my relationships. Any fire, no matter what size, can do unwanted damage. That's why the best kind of fire management is fire prevention. By the same reasoning, the best kind of anger management is anger prevention.

Traditional anger management therapy is directed at how to manage your emotions and behavior once the fire has started. Later on you also might learn to identify triggers, or sparks, that set you off into anger so that you can stay ahead of it. This doesn't mean that you have solved your anger problem. It just means that you have learned compensating strategies to avoid it and distract yourself before the destruction starts. The raw materials for combustion are still lying around for you to trip over.

Can you list some of the raw materials that will light a fire in your emotion instantly?

1. _____
2. _____
3. _____

These raw materials kindle our emotions that will start a fire in a flash! To quote Superman, "We react quicker than a speeding bullet and more powerful than a locomotive." As a Pastoral Counselor I heard many clients state that they have this feeling of "going insane or losing your mind." "Maybe I'm losing it?" "I have no control over my thoughts or actions." "Am I making a fool out of myself?"

Can you list some of the feelings that you have experienced?

1. _____
   _____
2. _____
   _____
3. _____
   _____

I have had many clients that are taking high blood pressure medication tell me, "I feel like fainting." This is a telling sign that the individual emotions are in bad condition. Instead of providing care for their emotions it is easier to take a high blood pressure pill.

In dealing with our emotional pain it is hard to confront the issues and the individuals that have caused the pain. The main individual is ourself. For some reason we just don't want to deal with our own stuff. We think it is better to stuff our stuff! We can place the blame on anything or others than to deal with the image that we see in the mirror each morning.

Not only does our body give tell tale signs but our mind will definitely tell on ourself. Within our mind we begin to alter the state of reality. We begin to get out of control often and more quickly. We express fear of most everything. We are afraid to drive. We are afraid to go places. We are afraid to make decisions. These are some of the signs of a person that is about to become out of control.

Can you list some of the times that you have gotten to this point?

1. _____
   _____
2. _____
   _____
3. _____
   _____

The mind continues to tell on us by allowing our thinking process to become obsessed about sensations. Our mind gives into having the ability to reason or be logical. Unable to think logically allows an individual to become out of control with their words and actions. Being unable to think clearly does not mean being insane. It simply means that the individual is not endowed with reason or understanding and therefore lacking usual and normal clarity.

So can you list some of the times that your mind has told on you?

1. _____
   _____
2. _____
   _____
3. _____
   _____

In discussing being out of control we must first learn what it means to be in control. Being in control of ourselves should not be so hard to learn or to accomplish.

Control is the ability to purposefully direct, or suppress change. Control can also refer to exercising restraint or direction over; dominate; command or to hold in check, including control over our behaviors both physically and emotionally. To be in control is to exercise authoritative or dominating influence over actions and reactions of our behavior.

We all have known individuals that we label "control freaks." These are people that must be in control of circumstances, events, and other individuals that are involved in their life. We have often mislabeled them as type "A" personality. Clinically, a person with this type of behavior is an individual with feelings of being inferior and having deep unresolved hurt.

Can you list some of the individuals that you know that are control freaks?

1. _____
   _____
2. _____
   _____
3. _____
   _____

82   *Who? Me! Angry?*

Now be honest with the individual you see in your mirror and ask if that person is a control freak too?

___ Yes

___ No

There is a need for control in life. Our Creator placed the Universe in form and control. He made man and place us in control of all He created. We continue to live in His controlled world. We are born and raised to be controlled and to control. One could say it is a give and take lifestyle. At times it is hard for us to control ourselves and yet we have a strong desire to control what others do.

Can you list some of the individuals that you have attempted to control recently?

1. _____

2. _____

3. _____

Can you list some of the people that you know or feel that have attempted to place their influence on you and control you too?

1. _____

2. _____

3. _____

What are some of the emotional feelings that are used in an effort to control another person? An example is using the emotions of guilt and coercion.

Can you list some other ways?

1. _____

2. _____
   _____
3. _____
   _____

Have you ever wondered why we all struggle over the "control issues?" Why do individuals have a need for control? This is not so much about how to control people as about their need for being controlling. The real secret is a deep need that people have for a sense of control. The "sense of being in control" is placing a person in their comfort zone. We all know that it is better to be quiet and let someone think it is their idea or their passion than to burst their bubble. By managing their sense of control, you can achieve far greater actual control. If you ignore this, you will soon fall into a power battle for control of the conversation and the agenda.

Can you list some other ways that you may get a better handle on the "control issues?"

1. _____
   _____
2. _____
   _____
3. _____
   _____

During my ministry as a hospital chaplain, one of the most disturbing things about having a terminal illness is the feeling of powerlessness. There is an unavoidable feeling of being unable to do anything about it. Being unable to control the illness can be even more problematic than the terminal illness. Perhaps the deepest need for individuals to have is for control. When we experience the "out of control feeling," we experience a powerful and uncomfortable worry or anxiety between the need for control and the evidence of inadequate control.

In painful and impending death being worried about dying may be more deadly than death.

From one standpoint, if we are in control of our environment, then we have a far better chance of survival. Our deep subconscious mind thus gives us strong biochemical prods when we face some kinds of danger. There becomes a fight or flight reaction and therefore we remain in control by taking either action.

The unknown and the lack of knowledge of how things work are the most stressful mental and emotional challenges that we face daily. We have a need for being able to predict what will happen. We as a group of educated people have developed what we call the "odd's factor." What are the odds? In the medical profession we want to know what are the odds of survival? Whatever we are told we instantly place ourselves in the most favorable group.

In the sports arena, we have fun with the "point spread." As humans we have the need for certainty and being in control. We have a need for understanding before we begin to gamble on all types of events and future things that are unknown.

Can you list some of the events and things that you have made a "predication?"

1. _____
   _____
2. _____
   _____
3. _____
   _____

Psychologist Abraham Maslow defined a need of hierarchy with the particular revelation that when lower level needs are not met, then higher-level needs will be abandoned in favor of shoring up the deeper needs.

Take a look at these needs from the Maslow pyramid:

Self-actualization
(Achieving individual potential)
Esteem
(Self-esteem and esteem from others)
Belonging
(Love, affection, being a part of groups)
Physiological needs
(Basics of human survival, food, water, air, clothing, shelter)

In Maslow's development of human needs he has also developed a pyramid in which these needs are listed and can be recognized as being basic to each of our needs.

For the most part, physiological needs are obvious what they are the literal requirements for human survival. If these requirements are not met, the human body simply cannot continue to function.

Air, water, and food are requirements for survival in all animals and humans. Clothing and shelter provide necessary protection from the elements.

Our safety needs take precedence and dominate behavior. These needs have to do with people's yearning for a predictable orderly world in which perceived unfairness and inconsistency are under control.

In the world of work, the safety needs manifest themselves in such things as with their physical needs relatively satisfied, the individual's safety needs take preference for job security, grievance procedures for protecting the individual from unilateral authority. This thinking has lead to the establishment of labor unions, disability accommodations and has savings accounts to "protect" our unknown future. Over the years we have produced and purchased insurance policies and have developed our saving for the "rainy day" mindset. The nationwide program of our Social Security system is one example of our need for personal security. Safety and security needs include: personal security, financial security, health and well-being and a safety net against accidents/illnesses and their adverse impacts

We have learned that the need for love and belonging are social needs and involve the feeling of belongingness. The third level of human needs after physiological and safety needs are fulfilled involves emotionally based relationships such as: friendship, intimacy, and our family.

Humans need to feel a sense of belonging and acceptance, whether it comes from a large social group, such as clubs, office culture, religious groups, professional organizations, sports teams, gangs, or small social connections family members, intimate partners, mentors, close colleagues and confidants. They need to love and be loved by others. In the absence of these elements, many people become susceptible to loneliness, social anxiety and clinically depressed. This need for belonging can often overcome the physiological and security needs, depending on the strength of the peer pressure: anorexic, for example, may ignore the need to eat and the security of health for a feeling of control and belonging.

We all have needs to be respected and to have self-esteem and self-respect. Also known as the "belonging need," esteem presents the normal human desire to be accepted and valued by others. People need to engage themselves to gain recognition and have an activity or activities that give the person a sense of contribution, to feel accepted and self-valued, be it in a profession or hobby. Imbalances at this level can result in low self-esteem or an inferiority complex.

Do you feel that you suffer from an inferiority complex if so why?

1. _____
_____
2. _____
_____
3. _____
_____

People with low self-esteem need respect from others. They may seek fame or glory, which again depends on others. Note, however, that many people with low self-esteem will not be able to improve their view of themselves simply by receiving fame, respect, and glory externally must first accept themselves internally. Psychological imbalances such as depression can also prevent one from obtaining self-esteem on both levels.

Most people have a need for a stable self-respect and self-esteem. Maslow noted two versions of esteem needs, a lower one and a higher one. The lower one is the need for the respect of others, the need for status, recognition, fame, prestige, and attention. The higher one is the need for self-respect, the need for strength, competence, mastery, self-confidence, independence and freedom. The latter one ranks higher because it rests more on inner competence won through experience. Deprivation of these needs can lead to an inferiority complex, weakness, and helplessness.

Can you list some of your needs for self-respect and self-confidence?

1. _____
_____
2. _____
_____

3. _____
   _____

Maslow also states that even though these are examples of how the quest for knowledge is separate from basic needs he warns that these "two hierarchies are interrelated rather than sharply separated." This means that the level of need, as well as the next level and highest level, are not strict, separate levels but closely related to others. This is possibly the reason that these two levels of need are left out of most textbooks.

What you can be, you must be. This forms the basis of the perceived need for self-actualization. This level of need pertains to what a person's full potential is and realizing that potential. Maslow describes this desire as the desire to become more and more what one is, to become everything that one is capable of becoming. This is a broad definition of the need for self-actualization, but when applied to individuals the need is specific. For example one individual may have the strong desire to become an ideal parent, in another it may be expressed athletically, and in another it may be expressed in painting, pictures, or inventions. As mentioned before, in order to gain a clear understanding of this level of need one must first only achieve the previous needs of physiological, safety, love, and esteem, but master these needs.

Can you list your self-actualization?

1. _____
   _____
2. _____
   _____
3. _____
   _____

Being out of control places a person on the score of 100 according to Campbell's Anger Flow Chart. Others may name it something else. Whatever one may call it, it is the tenth emotions away from being happy. I feel I must issue a warning notice as when someone becomes irrational it may be time to call for professional help. It may be time to call 911.

CHAPTER ELEVEN

HOT BUTTONS!

You have now learned The Campbell's Anger Flow Chart and are familiar with how to use it to your advantage. What do we do now? That is a great question and I will discuss it in the next chapter but for now we need to return to the mirror.

What do you see in the mirror what? List what you see.

1. _____
   _____
2. _____
   _____
3. _____
   _____
4. _____
   _____

No, I have not made an error by listing four spaces for you to record what you need to see in your mirror. For you will notice that there are more things in the mirror than just you! All this time all you have been looking at is you and those three personalities: me, myself, and I. For now I would like for you to look at what is at the top of mirror. What do you see? Look to your right and left and what do you see? Most importantly, look at what is behind you. What do you see? All these things have an influence on our behavior. This is the "stuff" that we see but we don't see. It is like our stressors and the other influences that we allow to be placed upon us.

Now, can you list what you are thinking and what you see emotionally?

1. _____
   _____
2. _____
   _____
3. _____
   _____

These are all in the background. Our life has backgrounds. These are things that we see but we don't see. They are there all the time but we just block them out. We have them blocked out because we are focused on the big "I."

These are what I label as "hot buttons!" We all have them. They are words, actions, events, and even thoughts that cause us to have the feeling of being upset and moving on up to being out of control.

Are you able to list a few of these hot buttons in your life?

1. _____
   _____
2. _____
   _____
3. _____
   _____

My wife and I have often talked about the words that made us get upset, mad and angry. Later we identify them as "Hot Button" words.

Matter-of-fact, I see these "hot buttons" as being hot pink, bright, and easily seen. Being much brighter and in reality, being more attractive than the old fashion "red" panic or buttons!

She was quick to share that the "you" words were upsetting for her. Words like "You" "You've" and "You're." I was quicker to share that it wasn't the words but the looks and crying that caused me to become angry and mad. We did not know but we were starting to identify some of the words and actions that gave us problems in our relationship. These are what we now call our "Hot Buttons."

Can you list just a few of these hot buttons in your life?

1. _____
   _____
2. _____
   _____
3. _____
   _____

Let's get started by looking at what you call "hot buttons." These are your "personal buttons" that will cause a reaction with the other person. Just in case you do not know what I am talking about (but for some reason I think you do) I will try to explain a little more in detail. Please note that while I am listing these three spoken hot buttons there are thousands.

We have been trained not to discuss politics and religion for fear of starting an argument. There are some people we fear because they give an angry response. So, we talk lightly with most relative and friends. *relatives*

In some households parenting is a moment by moment chore that remains problematic twenty-four hours a day, seven days a week. I will share some of the hot buttons of parenting. These are in addition to the major hot buttons that I share in this chapter.

Our children often times make statements that are hot buttons. One such statement is "I hate school." Children cannot see past tomorrow so they do not see that failing in school is a problem. Yet they know that education is important to the parents. This statement is an automatic invitation for a lecture on how the child is throwing away their future. This statement is a hot button!

Have you ever had this experience with a child? If so, how did is turn out?

1. _____
   _____
2. _____
   _____
3. _____
   _____

Another hot button that children use with their parents is, "I'm going to leave!" This often places the parent on a guilt trip. It makes the parents backs off from exerting his or her authority. The reason is that the parent fears what might happen if the child does in fact run away and start living on the streets. This is so problematic that the parent can't stand it.

Children know this and use this as an effective tool to paralyze their parents from taking action or enforcing family rules or consequences.

How do you or would you deal with a child that advises the family that they are going to leave home?

1. _____
   _____
2. _____
   _____
3. _____
   _____

While most "hot buttons" are pushed by starting a sentence with the use of: you, you're and you've! However, there are also two non-spoken hot buttons that I will share. Keep in mind that there may be thousands of non-spoken "hot pink buttons!"

The "you" word. That's right! YOU! The word "you" starts a sentence and most often a paragraph or more with a personal attack on a person in which you are attempting to communicate? You might not at this time be arguing. But the button word "you" will quickly lead to an argument.

Can you list some of the ways that the "you" word will cause you to become ready to argue?

1. _____
   _____
2. _____
   _____
3. _____
   _____

I have two children that are teachers in the public school system. I am told that to teach you must lead by leadership. Which is, I'm told, that if I want you to stop using the "you" word with me then I should be the leader and not use it with you and therefore, teaching you another way to communicate without using that word. Let me be the first to say that is very difficult to accomplish.

Can you list some ways that you can communicate without the use of the "you" word?

1. _____
2. _____
3. _____

One of the most used statements that is a family hot button is: "You never let me do anything!" This instantly invites the parents to point out times that they have let the child do whatever they want. This takes the parent off the real issue at that moment and gives the child the upper hand in the discussion.

Can you list some of the times that your child or children have used this hot button?

1. _____
2. _____
3. _____

Please note that the "You never let me do anything" hot button is spoken within a relationship that is considered controlling and abusive.

Can you list some of the times that an adult has used this hot button with you?

1. _____

2. _____
   _____
3. _____
   _____

There is a hot button that is intended to induce guilt and angry feelings and will make you question your self-worth. This hot button is, "You do not love me!" Unfortunately, as a parent, we take the "bait!" Instead of recognizing that love has nothing to do with the issue we instantly become in a rage! Parents often have to insist their child wear a coat in the cold when the child doesn't want to wear it. Parents are administers over the child when the child is too immature to know what is best for them.

Can you list some of the times you have struggled with these guilt and angry feelings?

1. _____
   _____
2. _____
   _____
3. _____
   _____

Since I am struggling with usage of the "you" word without it becoming a hot button, I am now attempting either not to use it at all or to only speak the word in a positive manner. I have been thinking that if I only use it positively or as an encouragement, then I might be able to avoid an argument.

Can you list some of the ways we can make these types of statements?

1. _____
   _____
2. _____
   _____
3. _____
   _____

The following are some "you" statements that I would like to share with you as what I call "The Stop Buttons!" "You must have practiced." "You did it." "You brighten my life." "You mean a lot to me." "You make me smile." "You deserve a hug." Wow! These "Stop" buttons I think will bring an argument to a stop.

As I said, I have been told to never say statements that start with "you," "you're," or "you've" however, I think these statements can be positive and helpful in dealing with people that try to get us angry.

The "you're" word! That's right! YOU'RE starts a sentence and most often a paragraph or more with a personal attack on a person in which you are arguing. "You're" is a word that is two words in one. These two words are "you" and "are" and when used together as one is spelled "you're" and has the same meaning as the two words used as individual words. They mean you are "blank, blank!" and "you're" blank, blank! It's what we place in the blank's that most often gets us in trouble and cause an argument and anger. The real problem is not these two words. The real problem is what comes after we say those two words as individual words or in combination.

What are some of your words that you place in the blanks that lead to an argument or a **flight**? *fight*

1. _____
2. _____
3. _____

Here are some of the words that we most often place in the blanks. We need to learn what they are and how difficult it is for others to deal with our outspoken charges. You're the worst person that I know. You're the Devil's son! Or you're the Devil's daughter! You're the meanest person on the face of the earth! You're kidding me! You're not going to do that to me! You're impossible. And the list can go on and on.

Can you share some of "you're" hot button statements?

1. _____
2. _____

3. _____
_____

Years ago when I was in the pastoral ministry there was a man that told me he had a good understanding of the Devil and what he was all about. Thinking that I might get a great sermon from him I had to ask him what in the world he was talking about. He told me that he knew the Devil very well because he had married the Devil's sister! Yes, I laughed! But that was just not right now was it? So far I have not found a sermon in his statement yet.

These are all hot buttons, words and comments that add to problematic relationships and increase the anger levels.

Can you list some of the words, or sentences that you have used the "you're" word and it has cause an argument?

1. _____
_____
2. _____
_____
3. _____
_____

Hot buttons are used to cloud our thought process and limit our ability to effectively enforce consequences. A statement screamed by a child at their parents like. "You're a liar!" is meant to get the parent to lose their temper through personal character attacks. Or a statement that follows in this attack such as, "I hate you!" will drive parents into a rage! If not controlled by the parent, these two statements will cause the parents to go from a moment of happiness to anger in a split second at 1800 mph and with an explosion in the home!

Have you experienced being driven from happiness to anger in a split second?

1. _____
_____
2. _____
_____

3. _____
_____

In a large number of our homes we have blended families. We have step-parents, step-children, half-brothers and half-sisters and step-grandparents therefore another hot button that we hear is, "You're not my real mother or father and I don't have to listen to you!" Now, the fight is on! A hot button has been pushed!

Can you list some of the times that this hot button has been pushed in your home?

1. _____
_____

2. _____
_____

3. _____ *delete*
_____

Now I will offer some defusing statements that use the "YOU'RE" word. I think these are all "stop" buttons. You're the best. You're special. You're talented. You're number one. You're learning fast. You're doing beautifully. You're on your way. You're a sport. You're doing fine. You're a pleasure to know. You're on the right track. You're a real friend. You're one in a million. You're a gem. You're delightful. You're a pleasure to know. You're improving. You're the greatest and you're remembered. The list can go on! Do you agree that we need to learn and develop how to use "Stop Buttons?"

Can you list how you think you may use some of these "you're" sentences in the near future? You may want to put a name to it to.

1. _____
_____

2. _____
_____

3. _____
_____

The "you've" word, that's right! When "YOU'VE" is used to start a sentence and most often a paragraph or more results in a personal attack that will lead to an argument. You've made me mad! Or you've made me angry! You've ruined my life! You've cost me everything! You've made me lose it all! You've cause me to lose my job! You've got me pregnant! You've made my parents angry! You've disappointed me! You've disrespected me! You've done it all wrong! You've never amounted to anything!

Can you list some of the "you've" sentences or paragraphs that you use that you know will cause anger and or an argument in your household?

1. _____
   _____
2. _____
   _____
3. _____
   _____

The following are some usage of the "you've" word that will keep you out of trouble and will make others think highly of you. These "Stop Buttons" will help in any relations. You've got it made. You've got it down pat. You've done fine. You've done it right. You've earned a star. You've got a heart. You've got the hang of it. You've got what it takes. You've made progress.

I believe that you now know that I am telling the truth about "hot buttons" that causes problems in our relationships and the "stop buttons" that may bring anger and arguments. May be [Maybe], we should continue to think of the "hot buttons" as being red in color and then think of the "stop buttons" as being seen as hot pink!

I have shared three hot buttons but there are two more that I need to make you aware of in our relationships. The fourth and fifth hot buttons are not spoken but yet they make our anger juices flow. These two hot buttons will get our attention and will cause all types of emotional reactions.

These hot buttons are so powerful that instead of making a statement or speaking a word the actions will speak volumes. These two hot buttons we learned while still in the crib! We learned these hot buttons, their demands and reactions that will bring instant attention.

Long before we could even think about forming words or speaking a sentence or paragraph these two "hot buttons" were developed to perfection.

The fourth hot button is the act or reaction of crying. Without speaking a word, making a statement, or giving a reason, your fourth hot button will explode! It will do it very well. We have had the practice from our days in our baby crib. Crying is an expression of our emotions. I can make the statement and declare that crying is the result of being sad or angry. Then only to realize that crying is the result of being happy and ecstatic. So which is it? You tell me! Crying is the most powerful hot buttons that you can use.

In my role as pastor and counselor, I often ask the following question to people when they were crying. It is so exciting! I never knew the answer or why. But the question that I like to ask is, "If that tear could talk what would it have to say?" I would like to ask you when you cry and if your tears could talk what would they have to say?

Can you list some of what your tears would say if they could speak?

1. _____
   _____
2. _____
   _____
3. _____
   _____

There have been many songs written about crying. Crying is a large part of the human experience. I have a friend that often sings an old song entitled "Crying in the Chapel." And then we may find ourselves crying in the prison too. We cry happy tears and we cry sad tears. Crying and tears are emotional traits that we know very little about. Why do we cry at funerals and then also cry at weddings?

Can you list some of the reasons that you cry at weddings?

1. _____
   _____
2. _____
   _____

3. _____
_____

Now can you list some of the reasons why you cry at funerals?

1. _____
_____
2. _____
_____
3. _____
_____

I had a minister friend that one Saturday started his day with a beautiful wedding and then hurried to speak at a funeral. His emotion that day was overwhelming.

Crying, which we also call sobbing, weeping, bawling, blubbering and shedding tears is a response to an emotional state in humans. Crying demands and requires actions or attention.

Can you list some of the times that you cried for attention?

1. _____
_____
2. _____
_____
3. _____
_____

Now I can hear the men that are reading this are saying that they were taught that men do not cry. I was taught that lie too! Remember that in this book we are looking for the truth. It is hard for us to realize that some of the things that we were taught as young children were just not true. I was a grown man before I came to terms with my emotions and the shame of a grown man crying.

One day I was reading and learned that the shortest verse in the Bible is a two word verse. The words are a report of Jesus attending a funeral. The verse reads, "Jesus wept!" Now I was in my twenties and I came to believe that if Jesus could weep at a funeral then it would be okay for me to shed a tear or two.

May I share a personal note with you guys? I delayed entering the ministry all because I was not able to control my emotions at funerals. I would have a tear or two run down my face at every funeral I attended regardless of how much I knew the person. It did not matter, I would get choked up and tears would start to run. I could not stop them. So I agreed with God and told Him that I was not cut out to be a minister because I would never be able to conduct a funeral.

Can you list some of the things that you know you should be doing but are not because of what you think someone might think about you or your appearance of being too weak?

1. _____
2. _____
3. _____

To help me with conducting funeral services I believe that God allowed me to conduct a service that would help me become more acquainted with that part of being a pastoral minister. My first funeral service came at the call of a funeral director with a body that did not have any known pastoral connection. This person had committed suicide after killing his girlfriend. I had no connection with this man or his family. But a minister was required by the State of Ohio to commit his body back to dust. It was then that I learned a lesson from above. His Spirit will teach you all things and bring all things to your remembrance. And I could not hold my tears back at my first funeral service that I was asked to conduct for a man I never knew nor his family.

Can you list some of the teachings that you believe you have received from above?

1. _____
2. _____
3. _____

Instead of crying as my wife did, I would sulk. How about that? Sulking is the opposite of crying but it works too. Just as well and at times maybe better.

Have you ever just sulked in your anger? If so, list some of the times as you remember them.

1. _____
_____

2. _____
_____

3. _____
_____

The act of crying announces a need. Crying also can have the meaning of abominable and reprehensible as in a crying shame. As the crying becomes more frequent and louder it indicates that immediate attention or remedy is necessary and is critical or severe.

We cry when we are happy. We cry when we are hurt. We cry when we are sad. And crying has a major purpose as it releases our stress.

Researches on emotional tears in the past suggest that when a person cries, tears carry with them all the stressful chemicals in the body. Emotional tears have high levels of manganese and hormone. When these chemicals are shed along with the tears drops, the person feels that their stress levels have come down and thus, it makes them feel better. That's the reason why we cry when we feel sad or hurt. It makes us feel better.

Can you list some of the times that crying has made you feel better?

1. _____
_____

2. _____
_____

3. _____
_____

Crying stimulates our nervous system. If you want to know why we cry when we laugh or when we feel sad, then here is the scientific explanation for it. When we feel hurt or really sad, our nervous system responds to these emotions by stimulating the cranial nerve. This stimulation of the nerves sends signals to the tear glands, through the neurotransmitters and hence, we end up crying.

Crying may cause a human bonding when a person cries. It is our way of showing that we are weak and vulnerable. By crying in front of our adversaries, we try to gain their sympathy. This might make the adversaries a little softer for the one who is crying and they may even end up as friends. People try to protect or care for the one who is crying, they are consoled, an attempt to talk them out of crying and thus, crying creates a needed human bond. This bond usually ends in a hug and comforting words that all will be alright.

Can you think of any times that you or someone else's crying resulted in you becoming a friend of that person?

1. _____
_____
2. _____
_____
3. _____
_____

Crying can be used as a manipulation and a way to communicate with others. Babies often cry in order to get attention from their mothers or when they are hungry. It is their way of communicating with the mother about their needs. Sometimes, by crying loudly, they manipulate their parents into doing things for them.

As a parent can you list a few times your child or children have manipulated you in such a manner?

1. _____
_____
2. _____
_____
3. _____
_____

Manipulation and communication behavior by crying is quite common in adults too. Men and women in relationships often resort to crying to manipulate their partners. This really works well as we are normally really good at this manner of communication because we have practiced all of our life.

Why do you think we cry and what does it feel like after you have been crying? Are the tears we cry when chopping onions are different from the tears we shed while watching a sad movie? What do you think?

1. _____
2. _____
3. _____

Tears are the liquid product of a process of crying to clean and lubricate the eye. Personally, I have taught that crying is okay and is necessary for an internal "cleansing." There are many reasons why we cry and weep. I am not concerned at this time with the research of crying. I just know that we cry at opposite ends of our emotional needs.

Can you list some of the reason why you cry?

1. _____
2. _____
3. _____

It is interesting as to why we physically react in the same physical condition for completely different emotional reasons. For this book and limited research, we will consider that we cry at different times for different reasons and to cry most of the time has healing for us to experience. I have had clients tell me, "I just need to go and have a good cry!" I will encourage them to do so.

Have you ever had some moments where you just needed to cry and if so can you list why?

1. _____
   _____
2. _____
   _____
3. _____
   _____

The fifth but not final "hot button" is what I call "The Look!" Without speaking a word! It is just a look! A look will speak volumes like crying. A look will remand pictured, in our minds for the remainder of our life.

A disgusted looks that sometimes include body language and gestures are very powerful tools that are used by our adolescents or our spouse to send us a message of anger. When we give way to these barbs by losing control, it gives a great deal of power to others and allows them to get under our skin.

Can you list an event or events when this happened to you?

1. _____
   _____
2. _____
   _____
3. _____
   _____

When is a look a look? I believe that a look is a look when the look is a picture that we find hard to remove from our mind. We often share with others times when they looked at us in a certain way whether it is for good or not.

These five hot buttons are areas that are your most vulnerable and others will find them and attempt to prey on them. Children have an uncanny ability to find these areas that bug their parents the most and apply pressure in that area. Likewise, spouses too have a similar uncanny ability.

There are hundreds of other hot buttons. I'm sure I have not heard them all. Some of the other ones are when someone starts their "preaching!" The anger level will increase from the very start of the first word of preaching when we "don't need it." There is a period of "walking away" or "ignoring" that will follow and feed the argument. A hot button has been lit and the argument has escalated.

Can you list some of the times that you have had this experience?

1. _____
2. _____
3. _____

Have you ever played the "Preacher" role? ___ Yes. ____ No. and If so, why?

1. _____
2. _____
3. _____

We often times will play the "labeling" game. Children will grow to hate labeling. I once knew a family in which the father became angry with his daughter and would shout, "All I want you to do is to become a decent person!" The daughter was so driven and hated this nagging statement that the last thing that she wanted to be was "that decent person!" She felt that she was never decent or my daddy would not be on me to become decent. So I'm not decent! She accepted the role that her father embedded in her mind and emotions. To this day her father has not been able to understand why she "turned out the way she is!"

Do you know of a similar situation?

1. _____
2. _____

3. _____
_____

Labeling can be especially dangerous because children eventually live up to these labels as they become a permanent self-fulfilling prophecy. Labeling also begins in the crib. Before the child can speak parents and grandparents thinking they are doing well will call their newborn "names" and therefore "labeling." The little fellow maybe called "bugger," "a bad boy," and the labels or numerable! While the parents are only labeling their loving child in "fun" the child will connect and will attempt to please their parents and will be that bad boy child.

Do you know such a child and parents?

1. _____
_____
2. _____
_____
3. _____
_____

With age comes a collection of criticism. Insults and criticisms cut deeper when they come from someone you love. This has a habit of damaging the inner spirit and like physical bruises will take years to heal if ever. So the hot buttons continue. We cannot keep them from coming. Therefore we need to learn how to handle and deal with them successfully.

Can you list five hot buttons that are important to learn to get a handle on and deal with in our life?

1. _____
_____
2. _____
_____
3. _____
_____
4. _____
_____

5. _____
   _____

It is not all bad for us to have our hot buttons pushed or for us to push the hot buttons of others. It is important to know to control our emotions. Keep in mind that we do not have a right to control any other adult. Likewise, they do not have the right to control your life. Hopefully, our life is in the hand of our Creator and not someone else. It is very important to be responsible for your own actions and emotions.

CHAPTER TWELVE
WHATEVER! – SO WHAT?

Whatever! So what? These are statements and questions of all questions and all statements!. Often times in discussion we answer with "whatever!" or "so what?" And the fight is on!

The anger levels are increased and we begin to have problems with anyone that is near us. What do I do now? I can now identify on the chart where I am in my emotions of being angry?

I can now practice and learn at what level I am. It's time to do something that will make an improvement in my life and for others. You may be thinking "so what" is next?

Have you noticed that most "mug shots" are not beauty or glamour pictures? Most individuals that have been arrested do not look too happy. I think we can understand why. But there are reasons why people are arrested and it is deeper than just the charges that they are being accused of committing. We can trace most illegal activities back to the issues of being angry. Again, most mug shot pictures appear to show people that are in pain. Emotional pain and physical pain is pain. Pain is pain!

It is no mystery that being simply upset will have an effect of your face. If fed with more negative emotions it will lead to back aches, headaches, leg aches, high blood pressure, high temperature, and at the same time we experience emotional and mental health issues. Anger is a triple header. Anger influences our emotions, our body, and our mental conditions. Anger I believe is what I would call a triune influence.

Age will take it's told too on all three of these parts of living. With age our emotions will be influenced in both negative and positive results. Some will become as we like to say, "They have a hard heart." Or we also like to state that "They are the kindest person in the world." With age our body does decay and is not as strong as it once was. Our mental conditions will grow with the wisdom that was once obtained life's experiences and the knowledge that we gain each day.

Can you list some of the changes in your emotions that you have noticed with your age?

1. _____

2. _____

3. _____

Can you list some of the lack of your body's strength?

1. _____

2. _____

3. _____

Can you list some of your mental changes that you have noticed?

1. _____

2. _____

3. _____

As we grow older we have been taught that we must take more medication to give us a better lifestyle in our retirement days. I think it all started years ago when we were taught by TV ads that we needed an aspirin every days. Then, we were told to take one in the morning and one at bed time.

We have been hit by a pharmaceutical tsunami. We have a special doctor for our high blood pressure. We have a special doctor for our back. We have a special doctor for our heart. We have a special doctor for our feet. We have a special doctor for our stomach. We have a special doctor for our ears. We have a special doctor for every part of our body. I know that these are very important physicians. If I have a medical problem I will be looking for the best and most talented doctor I can find. We even have doctors that are known as pain management physicians. What happened to the go old fashion M. D.?

I am not against medication, doctors, nurses or medical staff. I would not be alive today had it not been for some very special and talented medical care givers. However, if we were not so angry, I might not need those medical specialists. Have you ever noticed the conversation of senior citizens? It's all about their doctors and the medications that they are taking and the future or past medical appointment.

I could fit well in any senior citizen home or group as I have two heart doctors, one general practitioner, and a pain management physician. I also have vein doctor and wound doctor.

I am currently taking a cocktail of medications that consist of eight different medications with fifteen pills per day. I consider seven of these pills I now take needed because of past anger issues. Will you be that honest with me?

Anger issues cause heart disease and heart problems. It will cause need for stress relief medications. I hope that the more I learn to control myself and my anger the less stress I will live with, and the better my life will become. Yes, I must work on it daily. At times I feel like I am an addict, so how about you?

Can you share some of your medical needs that you believe will improve if you can learn to reduce your stress levels?

1. _____
   _____
2. _____
   _____
3. _____
   _____

As you continue to look in your mirror, I would ask you to now look at what is behind you. What do you see? For most I have found that we have a wall behind our backs as we stand in our bathrooms in our home. This is somewhat symbolic that we have a blank wall that we never see. Often in our life there is a wall that we do not see that blocks our happiness. Anger is a robber of happiness.

112   Who? Me! Angry?

Can you list some of the times that you know that you have been robbed of your happiness?

1. _____
_____
2. _____
_____
3. _____
_____

Matter of fact, I will also say that anger will rob us of our time, our talents, our finances and so many other things that we hold of value.

Can you list some of the occasions or events that you have allowed anger to rob you of yourself?

1. _____
_____
2. _____
_____
3. _____
_____

Now do you begin to see the complete picture of looking in your mirror? You are not the only object. Life is always changing and just as if we were to move into a different bathroom everyday and look in the mirror there would be a different background. We must never get used to our background. Always know what is around us daily as it will be different. I do not know anyone that experiences and lives the same life day in and day out.

Can you list some of your background that you now understand is changing daily?

1. _____
_____
2. _____
_____
3. _____
_____

There comes a time in everyone's life that we find that we must turn around. This may be one of those times. If you are tired of being angry and having others being angry at you, too, it may be time for a change or a about turn.

Can you list some of the changes that you would like to see?

1. _____
   _____
2. _____
   _____
3. _____
   _____

I believe that in the beginning God created everything and said three words, "It is good!" Humans were created in His image and at that time in history a perfect human. God did not create any faulty individuals. Our looks and our physical condition might not be what we want it to be but it is what He wants us to look and be like. So stop driving yourself mad with endless ways to improve, and just accept the glory of your being as He has formed you to be. Why do we think that we can improve what God has done?

Do you think that God made a mistake in what you look like? If so, list some of the things that you would like for God to have done differently.

1. _____
   _____
2. _____
   _____
3. _____
   _____

Is it good that God has not allowed us to help Him design what we look like or when we were born or to know our future? If you could have told Him what you wanted to look like what would you have asked of Him to give you?

Today we live in a society that is always looking for the "truth" in all events. For those who tell the truth they are "set free." In this act we can experience the real meaning of freedom! Freedom allows one to have purpose for living.

Have you ever wondered," What is one's purpose for living?" Today you woke up and for what purpose? Is it to help others? Is it to be dependent upon others? Is it to live and give? Or is it to talk and take?

What do you think your purpose for this day?

1. _____
_____
2. _____
_____
3. _____
_____

I have learned over my years of living there are two types of people, the takers and the givers. Which are you? I might need to draw your attention back to the mirror. The question and the statement of Who? Me! is one that we might need to address.

I once received a gift from a friend that I continue to enjoy. While eating lunch in the hospital cafeteria I felt a warm tender hand on the back of my shoulder and as they walked by I heard these wonderful words, "Have a blessed day." With a pat on the back and positive verbal blessing, my soul was lifted upward. After the person left the room I was left speechless and one of the greatest warm and, yes, fuzzy feelings you have ever felt in your life! No there were no ribbons, no Oscar Awards, but one of the greatest gifts of all! The human touch with a verbal blessing!

Is there anyone that you would like to pronounce a blessing upon? If so, who?

1. _____
_____
2. _____
_____
3. _____
_____

This gift was priceless even though it cost nothing! Why don't we become creative and give gifts without buying, spending fortunes, using the credit card or even cash? Why are we not giving of ourselves and our human touch? Why not give of our time, talents, knowledge, experience, true love without the commercials and no strings attached?

There are added values in giving of ourselves, such as, the value of memories. The most precious things in our life are memories. We are able to store both the good times and the bad times. But our file of memories no one can take away. Gifts are given and lost but memories remain at all cost until we die. Then our friends and family may have memories of us after we die. We cherish the memories of our parents and others that have died in our lifetime. Therefore, they continue to bring us pleasure as we think of them. We can live on after separation and death by the memories we give and leave to those that we love. Just in case you have any doubt, why do we take thousands of pictures of our family and friends at special times or for no reason at all? So, we all can say, "Thanks for the memories!"

Can you list some of the memories that you would like to say, "Thanks for the memories?"

1. _____
   _____
2. _____
   _____
3. _____
   _____

The need to control our emotions and anger could be so that those that we live with, play with, work with, worship with, and love will have great memories of who we are and have been during the time that we have shared with them. Go ahead and ask the question, "Who? Me!"

My three year old granddaughter already knows that when her friends laugh at her something is wrong. She feels hurt by her friends. Hurt by those that she has learned to trust. Again, in playing, daddy hit her with a snowball. The shock and the feeling of the energy within the snowball resulted in a facial expression of disbelief. How could her daddy do that? At 36 months old she is already learning that people close to you may hurt.

When we talk about early childhood development and hurt that go back to our childhood this is what we are talking about. However, with time being on our side hurt is forgotten. Or maybe it isn't? When her hurt is fed by other similar hurts and builds over time and in ten short years, and at the age of 13, she could develop issues of being angry "normally" and not knowing why?

Emotional hurt causes pain, an inward pain that may develop into an outward physical digamous of body pain. When our body begins to hurt we fail to look inward but we too often look for a quick external fix. This quick fix will often come in the form of medication. Most medication is nothing more than a "band-aid" and does not repair the cause of the pain. We are trained to take a pill for our pain and we are convinced that our pain will vanish in a flash!

Can you list some of the times that you have taken a pill for your discomfort and the pain almost ran away at the sight of the little pain pill?

1. _____
   _____
2. _____
   _____
3. _____
   _____

For years I had an ulcerated wound and have gone to doctors, they have fixed the ulcer and it will heal and close up and all appeared well. However, the ulcer would continue to reoccur. Four times I have had this medical problem taken care of and healed. I now have gone to a different doctor and a different approach has been taken. Now I am told that with laser surgery the ulcer can be fixed permanently. To get to the problem of my ulcer will require an intrusive procedure. In terms that I can understand I am told that I have a leaky vein that continues to leak and therefore, the ulcer will continue to recur.

I must stop. I must give way to making a change in my life. It may hurt for a while. But I am told that to fix my medical problem I must have it repaired from the inside out. That makes sense but I really don't want to have it done. Honestly, I must allow myself to face this painful procedure that will allow the correct healing. Likewise we must face the procedures that will allow the correct healing of our emotions and the pain that the emotional hurt brings.

Taking pain medication is an option and it requires a serious decision. We should be aware of the possible side effects from a single drug taken as well as the dangers of combining different medications. This is a decision that should be made with your treating physician who knows your medical history.

If we could use our "command horse sense" and just think for a moment about what is happening to us we might find some very unpleasant things that are going on within us. First read the side effects of any medication that your doctor prescribes for you to take. Have a good understanding of what your body and mind will do once you consume this medication. We must learn the truth concerning the medications that we take to help in the healing process and in the betterment of our lifestyle.

There was a time in our medicine cabinet that an aspirin was the strongest medication there and a person would have to talk the whole bottle to kill them. Now we have medications that only two or three pills are capable of killing. For some people the safe-deposit box at the bank is the safest place to keep their medications.

One of the fastest growing business' in America is the national chain of drug stores. This does not count the food stores that house a drug department and national retail stores. And of course there are still hundreds of mom and pop and neighborhood drug stores. I find it difficult to find someone that is not taking medication for some type of ailment.

I offer to you that most of our physical conditions begin in early childhood anger issues that have gone unnoticed and unresolved. These early hurts are fed for decades. We call this "baggage." Mix our unsolved early childhood issues with the built up anger of adolescence and by the time we become a young adult our baggage is almost unbearable One of my editors stated: "From a little evening bag to an overnight bag to a suitcase!"

Yes! This could be a part of the demand for teenage drinking and drug usage! Could this add to the continued increase in domestic violence? These are some of the issues that I believe could be rectified if our anger issues were dealt with in early childhood. I feel that by the time we wake up and have an angry teenager that is out of control, it is too late to begin successful counseling sessions. Most of the time it is too late.

Can you list some of the issues that you have dealt with in your family?

1. _____
_____

2. _____
_____

3. _____
_____

I have often seen and wonder what teenagers have to be depressed and angry about. Yet, our counseling offices are full of angry adolescents. For some reason we think that a pill will fix the child. The real issues are never addressed nor fixed. We now have adults taking "cocktails" of medications and angry as hell. Do you know anyone like this?

Can you list some of them?

1. _____
_____

2. _____
_____

3. _____
_____

Are you honest and truthful enough to place your name at the top of this list? Who? Me?

Let's move forward and be truthful. Our society has a major drug problem both legal and illegal. The truth is, most of us do not know the meaning of addiction and the difference between being addictive and being dependant upon required medications.

Can you list your understanding of being addicted to drugs?

1. _____
_____

2. _____
_____

3. _____
   _____

Can you list your understanding of being dependent on medication?

1. _____
   _____

2. _____
   _____

3. _____
   _____

Prescription pain medicine addiction grabs headlines when it sends celebrities spinning out of control. It also plagues many people out of the spotlight who grapple with painkiller addiction behind closed doors. Although widespread, addiction to prescription painkillers is also widely misunderstood and those misunderstandings can be dangerous and frightening for patients dealing with pain. Where is the line between appropriate use and addiction to prescription pain medicines?

How can patients stay on the right side of that line without suffering needlessly?

1. _____
   _____

2. _____
   _____

3. _____
   _____

I think that it is very important that we spend some time being truthful with ourselves, about ourselves, our family, and our household. You have already taken an inventory of your medications that are under your care and in your house. Some of these drugs are as dangerous as a loaded gun with the safety lock off.

I find it's very important to have you understand what an opioid narcotic is, how they work, the common side effects, and drug induced symptoms that may warrant medical attention. Please note I am not a medical doctor. I would encourage you at anytime to see your doctor for your medical condition and needs.

Pain is personal. No two individuals perceive pain in the same manner. No one can feel your pain the way you do. This is one reason why your communication to your physician is important to manage pain effectively. There are hundreds of drugs and other treatments available to treat your back, leg, neck, and all other pain. Managing pain does not have to be a solitary effort when you and your physician work together.

Does the stress in your life add to your physical pain? If so, can you list some of the stressors?

1. _____
2. _____
3. _____

For centuries opiates have been used to relieve pain. Opioids are derived from the seedpod of the poppy plant (palaver somniferous) are referred to as opiates. Morphine and codeine are commonly known opiates derived from opium. Other opioids include synthetics such as meperidine (Demerol) and chemicals naturally found in the body, such as endorphin.

How does this drug treat pain? Opioids work to relieve pain in two ways. First, they attach to opioid receptors, which are specific proteins on the surface of cells in the brain, spinal cord and gastrointestinal tract. These drugs interfere and stop the transmission of pain messages to the brain. Second, they work in the brain to alter the sensation of pain. These drugs do not take the pain away, but they do reduce and alter the patient's perception of the pain. These might need to be stated again! These drugs do not take the pain away, but they do reduce and alter our perception of the pain. So when we state, "my pain has gone" we are lying to our self!

Can you list the two ways in which opioids relieve pain?

1. _____
2. _____

Let's take a look at the factors affecting the "effects" of our medication. The effects of any drug depends on the amount taken at one time, your past experience with the drug, and whether the drug is injected, administered intravenously or taken orally. Your psychological and emotional stability may also affect the effect of the drug. Of course, combining drugs with other opioids or alcohol can produce profound side effects. Some side effects can be harmful or lethal.

Chronic opioid use may result in a high tolerance to the drug. This means a higher ability to develop a high tolerance for any and all medications is very problematic. Larger doses of the drug are needed to obtain the same initial pain relieving effects. Some patients develop a cross tolerance, which means that prolonged use of one opioid may cause a tolerance to develop to all opioids.

Can we develop a tolerance of medication? _____Yes _____No

Withdrawal symptoms may result when the dosages are reduced or abruptly stopped. The body adapts to the presence of an opioid. Symptoms of withdrawal may begin as early as a few hours after usage is dramatically lowered, and the symptoms peak two to three days thereafter. You should never alter the prescribed dosage or stop an opioid without the treating physician's knowledge and advice. This means taking more often and self increasing of the medication.

The symptoms of withdrawal include a craving for the drug, restlessness, moodiness, insomnia, yawning, abdominal cramps, diarrhea, and goose bumps. All drugs cause side effects. Some are acceptable and others are bothersome or even dangerous. Common side effects include euphoria, drowsiness, nausea, vomiting, constipation, dilated pupils, and respiratory depression. You should always report common side effects to your treating physician.

Can you list four symptoms of withdrawals from drugs?

1. _____

2. _____

3. _____

4. _____

We have come to believe that if a person needs higher doses or have withdrawal symptoms they must be an addict. In reality that might even sound like addiction to you but remember most people aren't trained in this area of life and it is too bad. This is not how the doctors define addiction. The truth has not been told and we do not know what the truth is or what to expect next. Anybody can become tolerant and dependent to a medication. That does not mean that they are addicted.

Dependence and tolerance don't just happen with prescription pain drugs. They may occur in drugs that aren't addictive at all, and they may occur in drugs that are addictive. It's independent of addiction. Many people mistakenly use the term "addiction" to refer to physical dependence. That includes doctors too! Doctors want to refer their patient because they think they're addicted, but really they're just physically dependent.

Addiction is defined by most medical doctors as a "chronic disease, that's typically defined by causing the compulsive use of a drug that produces harm or dysfunction, and the continued use despite that dysfunction." For example, a person who's addicted might have symptoms such as "having drugs interfere with your ability to function in your role or spending most of your time trying to procure a drug and take the drug.

Most doctors believe that physical dependence, which can include tolerance and withdrawal, is different. It's a part of addiction but it can happen without someone being addicted. It means that if someone has withdrawal symptoms when they stop taking their painkiller, it means that they need to be under a doctor's care to stop taking the drugs, but not necessarily that they're addicted.

Can you list three things that you have learned about medical dependence versus medical addiction?

1. _____

2. _____

3. _____

Some think that everyone gets addicted to pain drugs if they take them for an extended period or long enough. The vast majority of people use their prescribed medications correctly and without becoming addicted. If the usage of pain medication is used with responsible management, the signs of addiction or abuse would become very evident and their doctors should act upon that condition with that patient.

Some warning signs could include raising the dose without consulting your doctor or going to several doctors to get prescriptions without telling them about the prescriptions you already have. Being addicted means that your drug use is causing problems in your life but you keep on doing it anyway.

Trying to diagnose early signs of addiction in yourself or a loved one can be very difficult. Unless you really find out what's going on, you'd be surprised by the individual facts behind any addictive behavior. It is very hard to identify someone who is becoming addicted. When it comes to people who don't have chronic pain and they're addicted, it's more straightforward because they're using some of these drugs as party drugs. Things like that and the criteria for addiction can become pretty clear.

Most doctors will admit that it gets really complicated when you've got somebody that's in chronic pain and winds up needing higher and higher doses. You don't know if this is a sign that they're developing problems of addiction because something is really happening in their brain that's getting them more compulsively involved in taking the drug, or if their pain is getting worse because their disease is getting worse, or because they're developing tolerance to the painkiller.

At this point with yourself or with a family member, please seek professional help.

Do you know someone that is at this point in their life? If it is you please go ahead and be honest, tell the truth and list your name too.

1. _____

2. _____

3. _____

All drugs have risks. Our doctor's are good at medicine, recognizing risk and managing it, as long as we're willing to rise to that occasion. The key is that one has to manage the risks under medical supervision. One of the false belief, is that I am a strong person and I won't ever get addicted.

The truth is, in real life addiction isn't about willpower, it is not about moral failure, or sin. Addiction is a chronic disease and some are genetically more vulnerable because of their DNA than others. The main risk factor for addiction is genetic predisposition. In other words, do you have a family history of alcohol or addiction? Why do you think the nurses and doctors ask all of these same old questions? They need to know if you have a history yourself and if you're in recovery from that. Your genetic history would potentially place you at higher risk of addiction for any substance. In particular, you should be careful using the opioids for any length of time.

The truth is at one time prescription painkiller abuse was "rare" but it is now second only to marijuana in terms of illicit use. Exactly how many people are addicted to prescription painkillers isn't clear. According to the published U S Government data: 1.7 million people age 12 and older in the U.S. abused or were addicted to pain relievers in 2007' About 57% of people who reported taking pain relievers for "nonmedical" uses in the previous month said they'd gotten pain pills for free from someone they knew; only 18% said they'd gotten it from a doctor.

Don't share prescription pain pills and don't leave them somewhere that people could help themselves. These are not something that you should hand out to your friends or relatives or leave around so that people can take a few from you without your even noticing it. The old unlocked open medicine cabinet of years gone by has become a thing of the past.

Today the place where we keep our medicine needs to be kept under lock and key for the protection of all concerned. I know a person that uses their bank safety deposit box and goes weekly to withdraw a week's supply and pray that no one steals them. We may think that is better to do without.

Under treating pain can cause needless suffering. If you have pain, talk to your doctor about it. If you're afraid about addiction, talk with them about that, too. You have a right to have your pain addressed. When you're in pain, there's no risk-free options, including doing nothing. Some people suffer pain because they fear addiction, while others are too casual about using painkillers. I don't want to make people afraid of taking a medication that they need. At the same time, I want people to take their drugs seriously.

Can you list some of the times that you suffered because you were afraid to go to the doctor or you became afraid of the medications?

    1. _____

    2. _____

    3. _____

    The medical profession is between a rock and a hard place. No one wants a person to be in pain and suffer but yet they feel they need to give education and help their patients to not become addicted. Therefore, we attempt to control the medication by pain management.

    Most doctors don't get much training in either topic. We've got a naive physician population providing pain care and not knowing much about addiction. That's a bad combination. Patients are urged to educate themselves about their prescriptions and to work with their doctors. The best relationships are the ones where you're partnering with your clinicians and exchanging ideas. Talk to your doctor and if your doctor will not talk and take time for you, then fire them and get another. You, the patient, is in control of your medical condition. After all it is your life!

    I feel the need to include as much knowledge as I can to help you manage your medications and also to provide information that will encourage you to remove your stresses and to monitor you personal emotional, mental, and physical condition.

    Prescription drug abuse means taking a prescription medication that is not prescribed for you, or taking it for reasons or in dosages other than as prescribed. Abuse of prescription drugs can produce serious health effects, including addiction and death.

Can you be honest and tell the truth and list the drugs that you are taking that is not prescribed to you?

    1. _____

2. _____
   _____
3. _____
   _____

The following are commonly abused classes of prescription medications for pain: Opioids, Hydrocodone (Vicodin), Oxycodone (OxyContin), Propoxyphene (Darvon), Hydromorphone (Dilaudid), Meperidine (Demerol), and Diphenoxylate (Lomotil).

The central nervous system depressants (for anxiety and sleep disorders), and stimulants (for ADHD and narcolepsy) include barbiturates such as pentobarbital sodium (Nembutal), and benzodiazepines such as diazepam

If you are taking any of these drugs, you need to have knowledge of the side effects. You may need help with learning these side effects. Is there anyone in your household taking any of these drugs? Do you have any of these in your house? These drugs are both healers and killers.

However, some think that all that matters is the easing of their pain. Pain relief is the key. In truth, it's not the only goal. Most doctors are focusing on functional restoration when they prescribe any type of intervention to control a patient's pain. Functional restoration means being autonomous, being able to attend to their activities of daily living as well as forming friendships and an appropriate social environment. In other words, pain relief isn't enough. The doctors can give enough medication to put the patient out of the pain and they will sleep all day and night but there is no functional enjoyment of life. The pain is not felt. But the quality of life is gone. There must be a balance.

If there is pain reduction without improved function, that may not be sufficient to continue opioid pharmacotherapy. If faced with a situation where continued use and increasing doses without getting any functional improvement, there is no need to just to go up and up on the dosage. The plan needs to be changed. Remember, you know your body better than anyone else and it belongs to you. Be truthful and talk to your physician often.

There are some individuals that think because most people don't get addicted to painkillers they can use them as they please. Tinkering with you prescription and painkillers is not a hobby. You need to take them properly. There is a definite addiction potential. Therefore, use prescription pain medicines as prescribed by your doctor and report your positive and negative responses.

Although you may find that you need a higher dose, you shouldn't take matters into your own hands. Overdosing is a risk, so setting your dose isn't a do-it-yourself task.

Also, always tell the truth about how you have been medicating yourself. Your blood pressure and body temperature will tell on you as well as your urine and hair follicles. Your body speaks long before the questions are asked in most cases. The asking of the questions is simply to see if you are truthful. You got it! The simple truth! The truth will set you free.

The medical staff knows if you are truthful or not. Not being completely honest will hurt your chances of getting the proper medical attention. My dear mother told me when I was growing up that, "I could fool some people part of the time but none of the people all the time." I'm telling you, your body will give you away. Have you not seen someone your age that looks ten years older? They have been through more trouble, emotional and physical problems than you. Or your body looks ten years older than them! Your body doesn't lie. Ladies, I hate to tell you, sometimes you can't get enough makeup on your face to hide all of the tell-tell signs. If you do, then your neck will tell on you. And if you wear a turtle neck then your back, chest and hands will speak volumes.

Can you believe it, most of our physical pain comes from some of our negative emotional feelings of being hurt and angry? Please do not stop reading as the next chapter is the most important chapter in this book. As we continue to look in the mirror we are now getting to see behind our focal point and see what is behind the scene. Join me as we continue to look at the wall that is behind our back. Who? Me! Angry!

CHAPTER THIRTEEN

THE SECRET!

As you look in your mirror you see the individual that everyone else sees and those emotions that only you can hide or allow to turn loose and live freely as you face the truth, your truth! As we see the scene behind our backs in the mirror we see the wall. We all have walls. The greatest wall is not the Great Wall of China (nor was it the Wall in Germany) but the wall that exists within each of us.

So finally, here is the secret. It is the wall that is behind you. I will name that wall for you. I will give you three names for It. The names are the wall of Truth, the wall of Forgiveness, and the wall of Love. I live very close to Chattanooga, TN and I have fished in the Tennessee River many times. That body of water has three names too they are, The Chickamauge Lake, The Tennesee River and The Lake by the Dam. Therefore, why do we struggle in giving ourselves (our personal body of water) three names that encompasses our complete being?

At times, I feel I have a river of truth flowing within me. I feel I have a river of forgiveness flowing too. I also, feel I have a river of love. I am the same river but with three different names and experiences within. As this river flows our walls will attempt to dam it! However, without the negative behaviors, actions and reactions of ourselves and others that we allow within our lives, an overflowing of positive energy, emotions and education as we learn more about who we really are will bring more the dam can contain.

I am convinced we are able to control anger with truth, forgiveness and love. I also believe I will live daily with anger issues. Anger issues are similar to any other addictive behaviors. However, as of yet, there is not any recovery programs for our addiction to anger. I teach to recovery from anger you need to 1. Be Truthful (with yourself). 2. Be Forgiving (of yourself) and 3. Be Loving (to yourself)!

130   Who? Me! Angry?

These three steps will lead you into happiness and far away for any anger.

First, let's look back in the mirror. What do you see? Do you see a person that is honestly truthful with themselves? Do you see a person that is forgiving of themselves? Have you seen a person that loves themselves? It begins with you. As I have said before, "Me! Myself! and I!"

To tell the truth one must be honest, forthright to see and tell the truth. Telling the truth to others is always great but to be truthful with one's self is true honesty. Do you mind if I get personal for a while? We lie to ourselves more than anyone else does! Those three personalities argue daily within and about all things being honest and telling the truth to me, myself, and I.

It was reported that Mark Twain said, "A man is never more truthful than when he acknowledges himself as a liar!"

Forgiveness of oneself is the key to any type of recovery. Before we are ever able to begin to forgive others we must first take care of our own business. We must forgive ourselves and that is the whole truth and nothing but the truth! Now we are moving toward the secret! Forgiveness!

Forgiveness is a twofold action and is therefore a twofold reactionary event. Forgiveness is a must for ourselves and is necessary before we are able to offer forgiveness to others that we have offended. Forgiveness is reactionary in that we will accept or reject the offer of others when asked to forgive.

We have a history of building up walls for many reasons and at various times and because of numerous factors as we live our life. These walls we think will protect us from the unknown and from things that we do not want to deal with or face. I am always interested in a backyard that has a high private fence around it. What is in their yard that they do not want me to see? Who are they attempting to keep out?

Can you list some of the many walls that you have built up in your life?

    1. _____
    _____

    2. _____
    _____

3. _____
   _____

Can you share why you allowed yourself to build these walls?

1. _____
   _____
2. _____
   _____
3. _____
   _____

After forgiveness of ourselves we are then and only then able and qualified to offer forgiveness to others. We will discuss this later in this chapter. For now we need to learn and develop a true knowledge and understanding of what forgiveness truly is and what it means to be forgiven and to offer forgiveness. There is a reason why I used the term "to offer forgiveness."

All that is ever asked of a person is that we offer forgiveness. You are unable to make the other person to accept your request for forgiveness. Once offered, there need not be any need for begging. The mind, heart, emotional, and physical expression of making the offer to forgive is sufficient. Final, there is no need for anything else. There is no need to bribe a person, give gifts, make promises, or any other effort to "make" this person accept your offer.

Your offer of forgiveness is a gift. Just like at Christmas, a birthday or any other events the other person does not have to accept your gift. I once had a person that was so upset with me that they refused to accept a Christmas gift that I offered them.

Wow! What do you do? What would you do?

1. _____
   _____
2. _____
   _____
3. _____
   _____

I have also heard that person does not forgive if they cannot forget. And that you must forget if you are to forgive. Forgiveness is all that is asked and needed. Forgetting is not required. Matter of fact, you had better remember or you are about to have the same person do the same thing to you again and again.

Forgetting is of God and it is His work. Forgetting is not your work or your job. It was God that said He would never remember our sins anymore. God also said that He would place our sins as far as the East is from the West and remember them no more. So far, I cannot find where He asked his followers to forget the past and remember it no more.

So what are some of the problems that we continue to face daily that causes hard feelings and anger issues. Can you list some of the issues you have with hurt feelings and getting angry?

1. _____

2. _____

3. _____

In learning about anger issues we must learn what are some of the problems that cause a person to become angry to begin with? The following are some of our problems that lead to our anger. Some of these identifiable issues are also called the most deadly problems. These issues are so explosive that when anger is added to them we move into the "danger zone" and someone may get harmed and hurt physically or emotionally. As we look at some of the most deadly problems there is life changing knowledge and understanding that we need to learn.

A medieval theologian Thomas Aquinas, said that pride was an inordinate self-love. We already know that pride is an excessive belief in one's own abilities. It has been called the sin from which all others arise. Pride is also known as vanity. Pride has been called a desire to be important or attractive to others or excessive love of self.

Can you list any pride that you may have in your life and have struggles?

1. _____

2. _____
   _____

3. _____
   _____

Do you know anyone that is consumed with pride and can you list what their pride is?

1. _____
   _____

2. _____
   _____

3. _____
   _____

Envy is a desire for others' abilities, situation, traits, talents and status. You may think other people are so much smarter, more attractive or luckier than you. We see envy in most every advertisement.

Can you list some of the envy in your life?

1. _____
   _____

2. _____
   _____

3. _____
   _____

Hating other people and their ways for what they have whether it is wealth, prestige or any other things that they may have is an emotional jealousy or envy. Envy and jealousy has been described as "Love on one's own good perverted to a desire other men of theirs." In other words, thinking that the person himself or herself should have more even if it means someone else will have less because of him or her. Have you ever had this emotional feeling of envy or jealous?

Can you be truthful and list some of these events?

1. _____
   _____

2. _____
   _____
3. _____
   _____

To continue our deadly emotional feelings we need to look at "lust," know what it is, and how it affects our life. Lust is an inordinate craving for the pleasures of our body.

Lust may occur in two ways. First, it is contrary to the natural order of an act as becoming to the human race. Secondly, through being contrary to right reason and this is common to all lustful vices.

We all have heard that two wrongs don't make a right! To prove my point the following is a good example: When we add "Anger" + "Envy" = Armed Robbery. (Managing anger and all of the other negative emotional feelings such as envy, wrath and hate are inappropriate feelings of revenge or even denial and punitive desires outside of justice.) Living in possibly the most pampered, consumerist society since the Roman Empire we have grown accustomed to having it all. And if not, now "I will get it soon." We justify our envy as wants and our wants as our needs and therefore it is just a matter of before we have what we envy. And if not we have developed a deep excuse that we call depression. Deep depression will bring us to a level of frustration, madness and anger. We have now moved beyond our ability to manage our anger.

We are so deeply spoiled that we are able to move into a state of rage if we don't get our way soon.

Can you possibly list two wrongs that make a right?

1. _____
   _____
2. _____
   _____
3. _____
   _____

There are many things that tempt us into becoming angry. When others are not doing their share of the load or not paying their part of the bills. Some of these actions and reactions we are able to give a label to and identify what we are dealing with.

When a person is lazy and are what we call "good fer nuthin" we are in a relationship with someone that is "slothful." As it is the avoidance of physical or spiritual work or labor.

From the "Pocket Catholic Catechism" we learn that "sloth" is the desire of ease, even at the expense of doing the known will of God. Whatever we do in life requires effort. Everything we do is to be a means of recovery or deliverance. The slothful person is unwilling to do what they know to do because of the effort it takes to do it. Sloth becomes a hindrance when it slows down and even brings to a halt the energy we must expend in using the means of deliverance.

Can you think of anybody that are lazy and what we may call "good fer nuthin?"

1. _____
   _____
2. _____
   _____
3. _____
   _____

Laziness is being idle and wasteful of time a person has. Most people have a hatred and anger for those that are lazy. Often others have to work harder when working with someone this is lazy. Laziness makes life harder for everyone. It is like gluttony. It is a waste.

The seven deadly emotions lead to anger issues. Now that we are able to identify the issues and how they affect our lives we are able to gain control and to make changes and to manage our anger issues

The following is a true story of how two of these deadly emotions can lead to death. The influence it has upon those that life during the events of the day and those that are yet to be born. It becomes a multi-generational family issue that continues to live.

The two emotions in this event are anger and envy but this time in history it lead to murder and the death of two victims, a life sentence for one and the dead penalty for the trigger man.

It was July 14th 1911 which is now almost one hundred years ago the following events occurred and has affected over one hundred individuals and multi generational decades in my family.

There were gun shots fired and two men laid dead. One was a Deputy and the other one a local Judge. The local Judge was Andrew

Jackson Beatty. He was my grandfather that I never got to know because of the anger of two men that fired the guns that killed him and his Deputy.

I have always been very interested in ancestry and in learning all I can about my family and our history. It did not take me long to learn that my mother's father was a local Judge in Burnside, KY in the early 1900's. He and a Deputy while attempting to serve arrest warrants on two men they knew and considered them as friends. These two men decided they were not going to be arrested and had planned to shout [shoot] themselves out of Burnside and run.

My grandmother was left with one daughter and three sons to rear. And only four months later, being pregnant she would give birth to her second daughter on November 17th, my mother.

Because of the stupid rage of these two outlaws my mother was raised without a father. She said her mother always told her to, "Be careful something might happen!" Of course mom told me the same.

Mom talked about her father whom she never knew. Mother really missed a father daughter relationship and would speak of it often. Therefore, my father had to fill that void. We know that a husband can never meet the needs of being a father to his wife but Dad tried.

While mom's mother and she were very forgiving and kind Christian ladies over the years I grew to know there was some hidden anger issues within. It was very well hidden and did not surface often as they both had learned to control their emotions. Their anger was displayed as a hurtful pain more than any outward negative madness or rage. This I never saw from either of them. They turned their hurt into one of many of their wonderful assists.

I can still hear them say, "It will be alright, God doesn't make any mistakes." And then every time I would leave their sight I would be told, "Be careful." I would say, "Ok I will and don't worry I'll be fine!" And mom's last words to me were "but something might happen!"

As a child, teenager and young adult I could never understand why I was told this? I considered, it nagging.

To take this back to the next generation my grandfather's mother was married to James Beaty in Fentrees County, Jamestown, TN. They had two daughters born before 1860. According to the 1860 US Census his mother is listed as a "window." And I have found court records where James Beaty was killed in 1860 to confirm this statement.

At that time my great grandmother was left with two very young daughters. On December 25, 1866, my grandfather was born. Nine months later she also gave birth to a fourth child which was her third daughter. I am not able to find who their father is. This is my family "Mystery!'

Every family has a "mystery!" We all have skeletons in our closet! So, I can hear my great grandmother telling her children to "be careful something might happen!" It is only normal for this "be careful" statement to be passed on to the next generation.

So my mother heard the same statement, "Be careful something might happen!" And I have notice that my closing statement with my children is, "Be careful!" I have just given them the short version of what I was taught. Now I am a part of a multi-generational emotion of fear, anger, and anxiety that I have "dump" on my children which is now the fifth generation.

Can you list some of your multi-generational heritage?

1. _____
   _____
2. _____
   _____
3. _____
   _____

Before I get to the emotions of our secret let me talk about the true part of our anger management training. As we continue to look into our mirror what you see is what you get. We never look in the mirror except to see what is needed to be fixed. Is the hair done right? Is the makeup on correctly? Are our teeth clean? Is the dress or slacks the right color or do I look okay in this outfit? And of course the most lied about question in the whole world is after looking in the mirror we ask our spouse "Do I look too fat in this outfit?" Lie, lie, and lie again! Of course, the answer is "No dear you look wonderful!" And then we lie again when our spouse will seek confirmation and will ask the same question again and we will lie again too.

Have you ever asked this question to someone that you really trusted only to have known that they were lying to you?

1. _____
   _____
2. _____
   _____
3. _____
   _____

As we continue to look in our mirror, we know that we must make some changes with our hair, teeth, makeup or just to pick lint off our cloths.

Now comes a time that is most difficult, the moment of truth. For some reason we trust the mirror. We don't even attempt to adjust the mirror to make us look better. We just accept the image in the mirror to be honest and truthful to us. There is few other objects that we trust more than the mirror.

Any effort we may develop to grow and to make a recovery causes us to take the time to look inward with honesty and truthfulness to make a change. To make a true change it requires a true forgiveness. We know that this forgiveness begins from within. We must learn to forgive ourselves. This is a secret! Without our ability to forgive ourselves reducing and managing our anger will not occur.

While learning to forgive ourselves we will notice that there is a part of our emotions that will develop from within and this is great. We normally want to hide our emotional emotions by denial and suppression. This is an indication of an internal wall that we have developed and built over the years by emotional stuffing.

The view in the mirror will keep us humble. My major problem with the mirror is for the most part it only shows the outward appearances. What would I give to have a mirror that would look within a person and reveal the inward appearance?

To manage your life is to take control of yourself. I am amazed at the individuals that are so called control freaks and feel that they must control their spouse or other individuals that they are in a relationship with within their family and friends. Yet they are not in control of their own body, mind, emotion, best interest and time.

Have you ever known anyone that behaved as a person which was a control freak and how did it make you feel?

1. _____
_____
2. _____
_____
3. _____
_____

It has been said for years that "Time is on our side." Time does have a way of reducing our emotional high energy or high energy of emotions. And therefore, it appears that time is an element that gives us an advantage in our anger managing skills. While this is true there are other issues and one such issue is logic.

Logic equals reason. I have read in the Old Testament that we are to come and reason together. To me that is a time of debate and exchange of views and discussion of a subject using as my father would say, "Let's talk about comment sense." The being of any conversion or dialog will lead to the truth.

God has said "He is Love." Jesus said that He is "The way, the Truth and the Life." And God offers "Forgiveness" of all wrong doings. If this be true then we may be looking in all the wrong places for our solutions.

What do you think?

1. _____
_____
2. _____
_____
3. _____
_____

Do you have any other solutions for you to find an answer to solve your anger?

1. _____
_____

2. _____

3. _____

What do you think is the best resources for you to turn to for solutions for your anger issues? Keep in mind the need to deal with and to meet your personal truthfulness, personal forgiveness and personal love?

1. _____

2. _____

3. _____

As a parent, I always advised my children to tell the truth. I told them that when (not If) they got into trouble to always tell the truth. When trouble and problems arise they can be repaired, fixed and an attempt to make things right if the truth is told.

We as students of the Word and World events have never found the boundary of truth, because truth has its source and fullness in God. While the truth has many facets, they all originated with the Almighty.

Again while no person can fully understand all truth, it is still possible for us to know the Creator of truth. By teaching my children to be obedience, it was possible for them to be free from the destructive forces of the world. This is the starting point on the path of truth.

While being under the influence of anger there is no room for happiness. Most people that have any emotions are either happy or angry. It appears that there is no place in the middle. Some people have told me that they are "ok." Well, what does that mean? Does it mean that you are just there or here? Just to be without any purpose and direction. I don't have an answer for anyone that is in what they think is the middle of anger and happy?

What do you think about this?

1. _____

2. _____
_____

3. _____
_____

Finding true happiness and self-actualization has no room for depression or controlling anger issues. What is happiness? How do you define it" How do you increase it? Does true happiness really exist? To find true happiness is a very personal journey. Happiness is an emotional or affective state that is characterized by feelings of enjoyment and satisfaction.

The word "happiness" carries multiple nuances that have risen and fallen in significance through time and in diverse cultures and subcultures.

We all want to be happy. Most of our goals are meant to lead us to the elusive goal of being happy, but we don't always find it. At this point in our life we allow depression and anger to take over. However, the real way of living is to tell the truth, the whole truth and nothing but the truth! As we have learned by our studies and by our experiences the truth will set you free. To be set free is true happiness.

To identify the triangle phenomena we must deal with the following: The truth is both forgiveness and love. The forgiveness is both truth and love. The love is both forgiveness and truth. Therefore, we now have the presents of triune emotions.

The problem does not lie in the proclaiming of the truth, forgiveness and love, but in those who do not submit to it; and want others to think they are walking in them

Truth can have a variety of meanings such as the state of being in accordance with a particular one of the main truths in life is that: "Some people would not know the truth if they saw it in front of them!" Likewise, there are those that have been forgiven and would not know it if they saw it in front of them. And also there are those that have been loved and would not know it if they saw it in from of them. What a shame!

In my doctors office on the wall is a framed pain chart scale from 1 to 10. Each visit I must tell my doctor where my pain level is on the "Pain Chart." If you've ever been to an emergency room, I'm sure you have seen this chart. This simple chart will help describe the pain you are feeling on a scale of one to ten. Likewise, I have developed an anger flow chart for your review and to use it in the same manner. By using this anger flow chart for your review will bring you to a long tested events and actions that will help us to stay on target and will have us manage our anger and our life.

There are many easy ways to keep you fit, happy, and healthy throughout the year brings us to an understanding of anger and our emotions, physical actions and re-actions to the events in our life. The next page you will see my Anger Flow Chart for your review. Hopefully you will be able to discuss the chart and where you are at any time when in dealing with your anger management issues as you look daily in your mirror

The secret to anger and to managing your anger is: forgiveness, truth and love that will bring happiness.

Therefore, the secret to anger management is: to be honest with ourselves, truthful of ourselves, forgiveness for ourselves and to love ourselves. If we are unable to forgive ourselves how can we offer forgiveness to others? If we cannot be honest and truthful with ourselves how then can we be truthful with others? And if we cannot love ourselves how may we love others? These are soul searching questions that we must come to answer for ourselves. These emotional answers come from two sources: One sources is from within us and the second source is from Creator.

I am not sure that there is but one main truth in life and that is: "Some people would not know the truth if they saw it in front of them." If one believes that God is truth, God is love, and God is forgiveness then where is God in our life? So, is it no wonder that some people do not see God in their mirror?

There appears to be a truinial line of emotions with anger, depression, and pain. Any pain without physical injury maybe caused by emotional hurt and is just as painful as a cut or broken bones. We call it depression and stress.

Reflecting on my father who only had a 1915 third grade education which carried him though his life until he died at the age of eighty. He would say and evaluate life's situation by logic and common sense. So let us come and reason together is an effort to use both logic and common sense to an issues. In our case it would be the issue of anger. There are three words that will stop anger in its track and they are: "I am sorry!" The statement of "I am sorry" will render the truth. Forgiveness will follow and love is shared. We know the answer for anger is: "Forgiveness," "Truth" and "Love!"

Be patient as in Ecclesiastes 3:1 we learn to… "Be patient, as to everything there is a season."

Now as you move forward, be patient with your emotional change in life. An emotional change will not happen overnight. After all, most of us have years of experience with negative anger, emotional action, and reactions so why would we expect to simply read a book and answer some questions that we are fixed? Just as if we take a pill and think that we are fixed. To be "fixed" takes a cognitive change in thinking, our emotions and physical responsive. In other words, it takes knowledge and hard work to fix it yourself.

No one else is able to do it for you!

CAMPBELL'S ANGER FLOW CHART:

By: Dr. Jerry Campbell

											O
											U
											T
			F							I	O
			R							R	F
			U							R	
			S							A	C
		M	T	A						T	O
H	U	I	R	F		A	F		I	I	N
A	P	F	A	R		N	I	R	O		T
P	S	F	T	A	M	G	G	A	N		R
P	E	E	E	I	A	E	H	G	A		O
Y	T	D	D	D	D	R	T	E	L		L

0 5 10 15 20 25 30 35 40 45 50 55 60 65 70 75 80 85 90 95 100

                                                        DANGER ZONE

Please Note: Living within the anger range from 60 to 100 is living in the "Danger Zone." Anger is one letter away from "D"anger. From the anger level of anger, fight, rage, out of control and irrational an individual is capable of being hurt or hurting others. This is the zone that causes abuse and domestic violence.

    Footnote: Campbell's Anger Flow Chart is protected by copyright of 2010, by Rev. Dr. Jerry Campbell Ministry, Who Me Institute, and CAMCO Production at 108 White Oak Street Rossville, GA 30741. E-mail address: revdrjerrycampbell@yahoo.com. All rights are reserved. Any reproduction and use of this material without the written permission of the copyrighter is prohibited.